Remarkable Women of Clinton County

I0806143

Remarkable Women of Clinton County

Anastasia L. Pratt

The History Press

Published by The History Press
Charleston, SC 29403
www.historypress.net

Copyright © 2015 by Anastasia L. Pratt
All rights reserved

Front cover, top (left to right): General McPeak's wife (sadly not listed by her first name). *Clinton County Historian's Office*; Robin Caudell. *Clinton County Historian's Office*; Jean Arthur. *Public domain image available through Wikimedia Commons.*
Front cover, bottom: Women at the 150th commemoration of the Battle of Plattsburgh. *Clinton County Historian's Office.*
Back cover: Camp Tapawingo, Girl Scout camp. *Author's collection.*

First published 2015

Manufactured in the United States

ISBN 978.1.62619.845.6

Library of Congress Control Number: 2014955130

Notice: The information in this book is true and complete to the best of our knowledge. It is offered without guarantee on the part of the author or The History Press. The author and The History Press disclaim all liability in connection with the use of this book.

All rights reserved. No part of this book may be reproduced or transmitted in any form whatsoever without prior written permission from the publisher except in the case of brief quotations embodied in critical articles and reviews.

This book is dedicated, with love, to a remarkable woman, Gloria Cusson Pratt, my mom.

CONTENTS

ACKNOWLEDGEMENTS

I am grateful to the network of people who shared photos and answered questions about the many women who have influenced life in Clinton County. Among them are Ellen Adams, Barb Benkwitt, Cecilia Esposito, Geri Favreau, Amanda Shannon Frennier, Patricia Hammond, Helen Anders Kho, Holly Kipp, Christine LaMar, Pam Meyers, Jennifer Moore, Helen Nerska, Beth Nolland, Willow Nolland, Kristi Spissinger O'Connor, Anne Hensel Ringuette, Eileen Roach, Kathleen Roach, Kelly Julian Sexton, Dan Shannon, Paul Shannon, Jessica Spissinger and Michelle Duprey Timmons. Maria Arce, Kate Dermody and Sue Orrell, my friends and colleagues, made my life easier while I was writing this, for which I am extremely thankful. Finally, I am incredibly fortunate to have a loving and supportive family, without whom none of this would have been possible.

INTRODUCTION

In 1998, events across New York commemorated the 150th anniversary of the Seneca Falls Convention and the many achievements of women throughout the state. One event, a statewide torch relay—beginning in Buffalo on September 15 and ending in Battery Park City, Manhattan, on September 20—was conducted as part of the Governor's Commission Honoring the Achievements of Women. As part of the commemoration, runners carried a torch across the state, "stopping to celebrate the Women's Rights anniversary with events such as the dedication of new historic markers," according to the *Press-Republican* on September 9, 1998. The stops along the way were Rochester, Syracuse, Plattsburgh, Binghamton, Watertown, Utica, Troy/Albany and Hyde Park/Val Kill. New historic markers in memory of "local pioneering women" were dedicated during the Clinton, Franklin and Essex County stops, and an outdoor ceremony, with Gail Judson as keynote speaker, was held outside the Angell College Center in Plattsburgh. During the ceremony, Senator Ronald Stafford recognized "the contribution of local women of distinction." After the ceremony, the two-mile relay continued, with Clinton County district attorney Penelope Clute, feature WPTZ anchor Stephanie Gorin, PSU student athlete Katie Castine and Seton Catholic track coach Gail Porcelli carrying the torch.

Those events were important, but they exposed a major gap in the local historical record. Major accounts of Clinton County's past, including the very important *History of Clinton and Franklin Counties, New York*, only mention women in passing, often identifying them by their husbands'

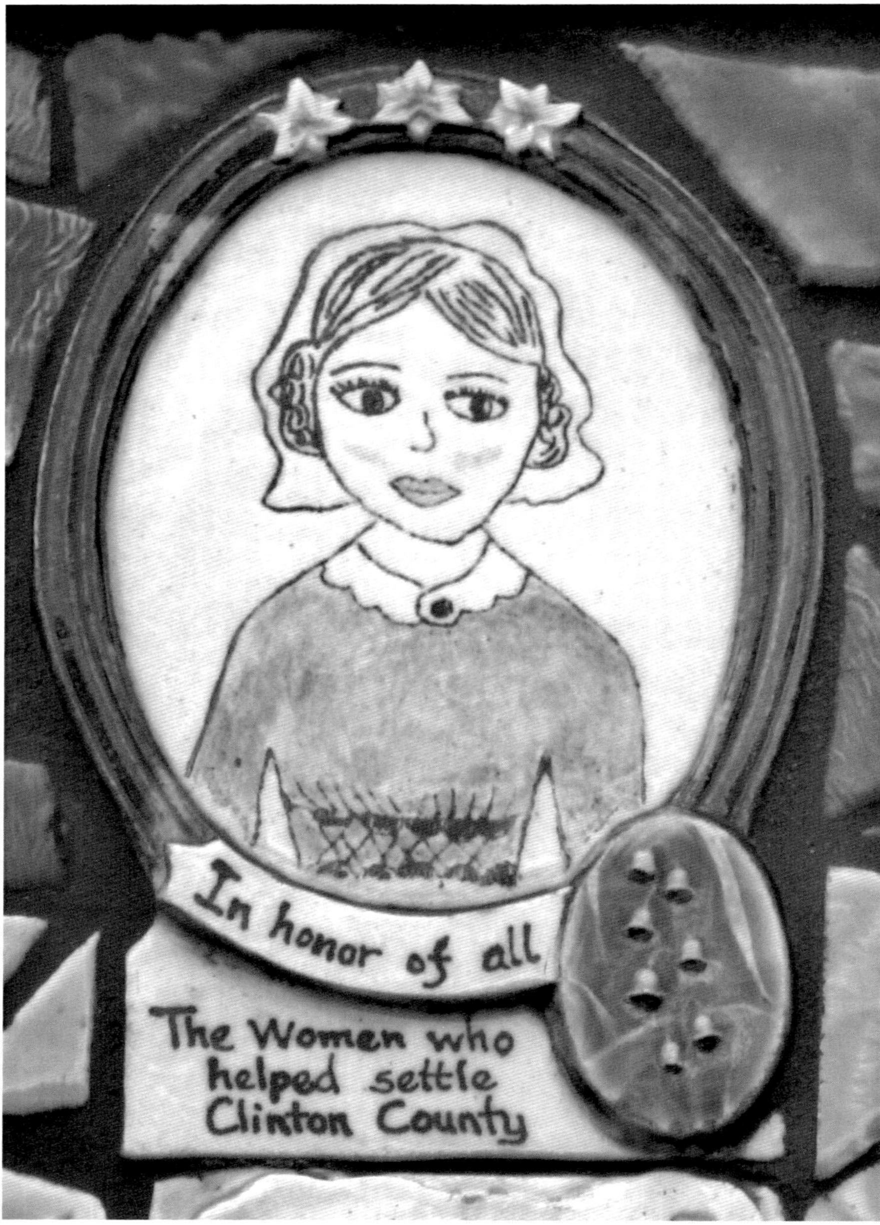

Detail of the *Clinton County History Through the Eyes of Its Children* mosaic, 2008. *Author's collection.*

names. In response, historians across the county worked to gather the names of women whose achievements set them apart and to propose some women for special recognition. Their efforts were partially successful: after 1998, the listing of women who were elected to governmental positions was more complete and a historic marker dedicated to Dr. Lucy Hobbs Taylor was erected in Ellenburg. Slowly, accounts of local history identified women by their first names.

However, a great many women continued to be left out of the historic record. Women like Emma Racette, who, her obituary explains, "will be remembered by friends and family for her love of children, her good cooking, her wonderful green thumb with plants and flowers, and her devotion to her husband and family," and Claire Hewitt, who, at the age of sixteen, "left school to join a group of Plattsburgh women who went to Washington, D.C., to aid in the war effort" and returned to Plattsburgh only after World War I ended, are largely absent from standard histories of the county. So, too, are the women who settled in this place with Count Charles de Fredenburgh and his workmen in the 1760s and the women who accompanied Zephaniah Platt and his associates to the area in the 1780s. The enslaved women who lived and worked in Clinton County appear only in official listings of slaves or in recordings of sale or manumission, while First Nations women rarely appear in any history of the region.

That reality became blindingly obvious in 2008 and 2009, when a group of students from across the county worked on a large-scale mosaic project to commemorate the 400th anniversary of Samuel de Champlain's arrival in North America. Each school district was assigned a portion of the county's history to research, beginning before European contact and continuing through the end of the nineteenth century. Their research, assisted by their teachers, local historians and the project organizers, led to drawings of scenes and objects that evoke the history of the area, while the drawings then led to the creation of ceramic tiles that would constitute, collectively, the mosaic.

In every instance, whether we were discussing early settlement in the region by men like William Gilliland and Jean Laframboise in the 1760s or the later settlement by men like the Platts and Benjamin Mooers, women were not mentioned. Accounts of the Battle of Valcour (1776) and the Battle of Plattsburgh (1814) occasionally mention women, though their contributions to the cause are minimized. Though they have always relied on women, the industries of the region—which have included everything from gristmills to shirt factories, retail shops to warehouses—were also largely silent on the contributions of women to the region. In fact, the only accounts that offered a significant discussion of women and their role in establishing Clinton County as a place of importance were those that focused on women as teachers.

Those glaring absences must be corrected. While this volume does not do the entire job, it does begin to fill in the holes, telling the stories of specific women of note and listing the names of other women who engaged in similar activities and belonged to comparable organizations. The names and stories of the remarkable women included here were gathered through careful readings of newspapers, local histories, correspondence addressed to the office of the Clinton County historian, photographs, anecdotes shared by others interested in correcting these omissions, letters, diaries, scrapbooks and published accounts of life in the past. Obituaries, anniversary notices, and wedding announcements have been particularly useful in this endeavor, as they offer a more personal look at women whose lives are otherwise invisible in the public record.

In order to share the stories of as many women as possible, I had to make difficult choices. First, I elected not to include women who are identified only by the names of their husbands. While they are, of course, as important as any other women, their identities have been lost in the recording of names. When possible, I have searched for the given names of those women and included them here. If that was not possible, I chose to list instead women with similar stories or engagements whose names were available. Second, as much as I wanted to include every woman who ever lived, worked or studied in Clinton County in this account, I had to narrow down my choices. For every woman mentioned here, there are dozens, if not hundreds more who have held similar jobs, participated in the same groups, studied at these schools and proved their merits in the identical ways. That they cannot all be honored here is heartbreaking. I hope that this account of Clinton County's past will inspire others to gather and preserve the stories of women, further celebrating the role that women have played in this region.

Chapter 1

LIFE AT HOME

For most of our past, the details of women's lives were not recorded. The conversations they had, games they played and books they read are mostly lost to the ages, as are their feelings on getting married, having children and grandchildren and experiencing the loss of loved ones. However, a few women, through their letters and diaries, and others, through newspaper accounts of their lives and deaths, help to correct that record.

Girlhood and Womanhood

Sometimes a woman's life was recorded only after her death. That was certainly the case of William Gilliland's daughter Jane, who died in 1766 as the result of a boating accident. In his journal, which was edited and published by David Martin, Gilliland describes the ordeal of witnessing the accident, recovering her body, laying it out and burying it near his house in Plattsburgh. He writes in great detail on May 13 that she was:

> *aged 6 years wanting 12 days, and the wonder of her age for Beauty, Stature, Politeness, discretion, Education, propriety of Language, Sweetness of temper, Gracefullness of address, strength of Genius & memory & above all for Charity and every other Virtue, never having Shewed the Reverse by either word or action—ever generous & Benevolent—Her Sudden Death Struck all her acquaintance with the most Serious affliction,*

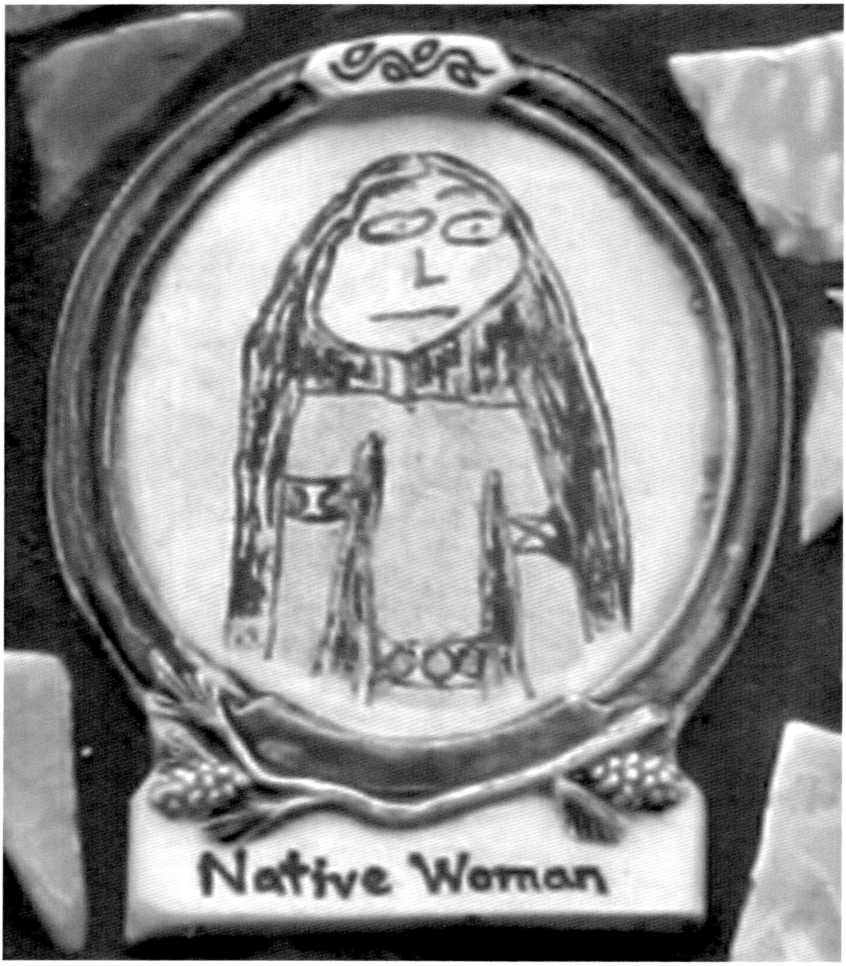

Mosaic tile honoring the First Nations women who lived and traveled through Clinton County. *Author's collection.*

> *was as generally Lamented as was her acquaintance extensive—many who never had seen her, who only knew her Character bewailed her Death with Tears in their Eyes—how* ["much" crossed out] *poignant then must have been the Loss of so Lovely a Child to her fond parents as well as to her Grand Mother and other Relations,—But great is our Consolation in the Steadfast hopes of her having made a hapy Change, & that thro Christs rightiousness & Mercy she is now glorifying her and our God—our Glorious Redeemer and his ever Blessed mansions above—*

One memorable woman from Champlain was Hulda Bredenberg. Born in 1899, Hulda graduated from the Albany Business College and then worked in a variety of businesses, including J.E. Harroun and Son of Watertown and the Wall Street investment firm Higginson and Co. Later she managed the offices of the Ski Manufacturing Company, which her brothers Oscar and Henrik started in the early 1900s, and served as a secretary in the engineering department of the Sheridan Iron Works in Champlain. When she was in her forties, Hulda married Charles "Woody" McLellan after the couple saved money every week for two years in order to provide for their honeymoon and for regular weekend trips after their marriage. By all accounts, the couple, who are noted for their work documenting the tombstones of dozens of local cemeteries, were quite happy, though they maintained separate homes until 1967, after Hulda's mother and Woody's father had passed away. Their years together, as described by Allen Everest, were filled with travel: "By making special arrangements at their respective houses, they were able to plan their weekends together, forgetting their responsibilities and enjoying each other's company when in many ways they were at their best. Sometimes they visited friends; more often they spent the time at a country inn and explored the surrounding area or, just as often, recorded gravestones."

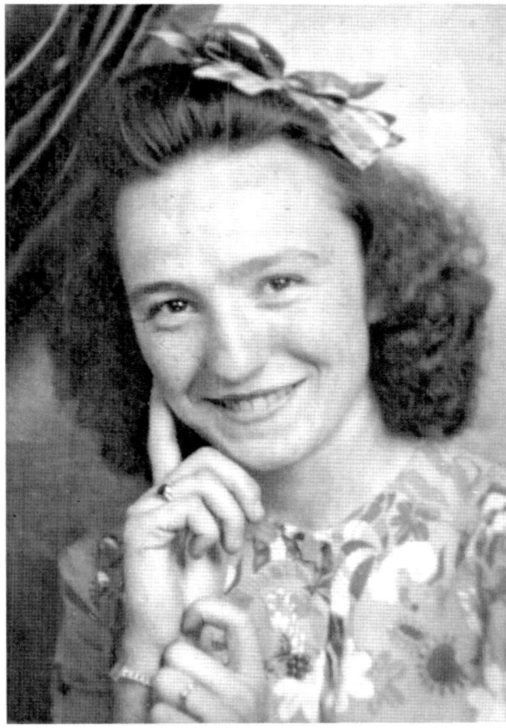

Beulah C. Laurin, from Chazy, was devoted to her husband, Marcel, and her family. *Marcel Laurin.*

Hulda's sister Mabel Bredenberg Woods was equally memorable. A 1917 graduate of the Crane Institute of Music in Potsdam, she was an English and music teacher, as well as organist and choir director, until the 1980s. Helen Anders Kho, who taught music in the area, writes that the Bredenberg sisters "would take my daughter and her friends for a whole day at a time and they would bake, sew, sing and dance the native Swedish folk songs of their childhood." Their mother was notable, too, skiing well into her nineties.

Getting Married, Being a Wife, Losing a Husband

One of the earliest accounts of a Clinton County marriage was preserved by Mrs. J.F. Gilbert, who related the story of her grandmother's marriage and early married life for the *Reminiscences of Old Chazy*. Gilbert explains that two years after Septa Fillmore and Eunice Edgerton married in 1797, Septa set out for Chazy; the next year, Eunice followed from Connecticut, with "her father bringing her as far as Middlebury, Vt., in a sleigh and grandfather meeting her there. They were both from homes of comfort and perhaps luxury at that time. Leaving brothers and sisters and a father's home to make a home in Chazy, then called the Five Nations, and almost a wilderness, I have heard grandmother say that if her father had known to what hardship and privation she was coming, he would never have given his consent." Continuing, she wrote, "With the woods and wild beasts around them, grandmother was sometimes left alone for two or three days when grandfather was obliged to go to mill, taking his grist and that of his neighbors to Chazy Landing and from there in a canoe to Aux Nois where there was a windmill. She would take her two babies up the ladder nights and pull it up after her, as there was only a blanket for a door below and the wolves were so plenty they lighted pine knots to keep them away. (The people carried torches when they went out at night.) One can imagine there could be little sleep for a mother with little children under such circumstances." During the War of 1812, when the British marched through Clinton County and engaged the Americans in the Battles at Plattsburgh, Edgerton, "frightened at the fearful hooting and howling at night," packed up her children and headed south, eventually reaching Peru. In her flight, "she piled bedding, clothing and several little children on a big wagon and sent them on ahead. Then she took other things and followed leaving her house filled with supplies of all kinds and all that they had gathered together in the few years of married life."

Many accounts of weddings were limited to simple statements: Abigail Douglass of Chazy married John L. Fouquet; Eliza married Judge Levi Platt; Elizabeth Smith, daughter of Colonel Melancton Smith and granddaughter of Judge Melancton Smith, married an army officer and traveled. In his September 13, 1807 letter to his parents, maintained by the Department of the Army, however, William Beaumont describes his brother Samuel's wedding in impressive detail. "Honored Father," he writes:

> *At 12 o'clock the procession proceeded to arrive in the following manner. The Groom and Bride paraded in front of a number of respectable Gentlemen and Ladies and moved a few rods to the hall (or store where the dinner was prepared) there they were received by the politeness of a number of Gentlemen (chosen officers of the day) accompanied by a Clarinet and Violin. After a pleasant regale the Groom and Bride with the rest of the Ladies were escorted back to the house from whence they came and there spent the remaining part of the day in social Chat—whilst the Gentlemen paraded and marched around—Commanded by Mr. Tyler, (commander in Chief of the Day). The scene was closed by the firing of Fifty-sixes, giving of toasts and huzzahing of Cheers—A short evening exercise was performed besides—the two people that were thus joined appear to be on the summit of love and enjoy each other's company to the utmost perfection and pleasure. She has ever treated me with the kindness of a mother and the affection of a sister. She has two of the finest children by her first husband who do her and him honor by their good conduct.*

Interestingly, despite his apparent affection for his new sister-in-law, Beaumont never identifies her by name, only acknowledging that she was a "young widow, sister of Mr. Tyler his partner in Trade." When, six years later, Samuel died of pleurisy, John F. Freligh left it to the elder Beaumont to tell his daughter-in-law that she was, for the second time, a widow.

The women of the Delord family—Elizabeth, her daughter Frances and her granddaughter Frances—all left letters (many gathered into a book by Virginia Burdick) and diaries that describe their feelings for their respective husbands and the events of their lives. According to Allan Everest, who organized many of those records into a historical account of the family, "a deep bond of affection, if formal by modern conceptions, developed between this man [Henry Delord] and a bride [Elizabeth 'Betsey' Ketchum] who was almost young enough to be his daughter. She matured rapidly and developed a dignity and self-reliance that served her well in the role of one of the area's leading hostesses. Yet without children they tended to develop separate lives, Henry with his growing public and private commitments outside his home, and Betsey with her numerous family connections and

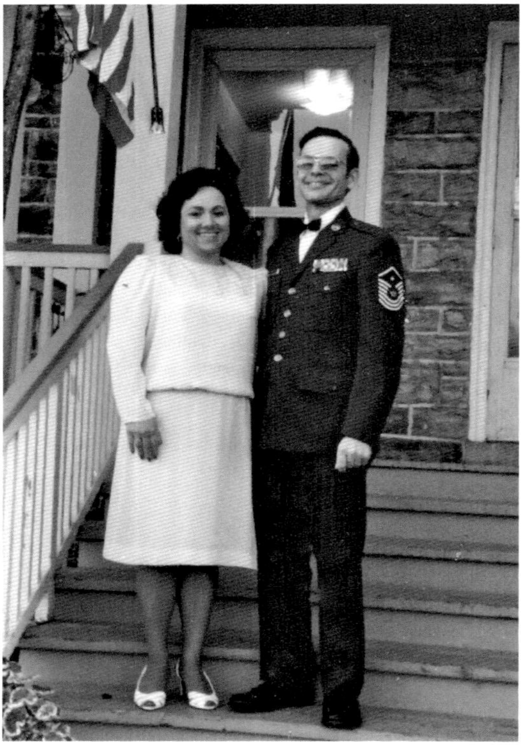

Janice and Paul Shannon, standing in front of the "Graystones," Chief's Row on PAFB, 1985. *Paul A. Shannon.*

the frequent trips they made possible." On one trip, which involved a steamboat ride on the Hudson River in 1808, Betsey wrote to Henry: "We move'd [*sic*] with astonishing Rapidity, had a pleasant time, everything on board in stile [*sic*]; if you had been with me I should have enjoyed myself highly." The year before, when Henry was away, her letter shows her love and concern for her husband: "I hope ere this you are safely arrived at Waterford. Im [*sic*] very anxious to hear from you and your not being well when you left home make me more so. I hope you will not venture to New York unless the sickness is much abated." Similarly, in 1808, she writes, "I am extremely anxious, my dear Husband, to see you and am waiting with the greatest impatience for the time to come that will again put me in your arms. Ma is here and young Miss Eleanor Sally. I have not been alone one day since you went away. I hope you will hasten as soon as possible." Clearly, the love and company of others could not compare to that of her husband.

In 1835, when Henry died, Betsey's grief was palpable in her letter to his sister Julia. "My dear sister," she begins, "How shall I communicate to you the sad sad tidings which has made me a mourning and disconsolate widow and your dear niece a fatherless child. Just at the moment we were anticipating the fond Idea of meeting you in the spring our hopes and expectations were cut off by the messenger of death, but it was the will of god and we ought not to murmur. He was the most tender and affectionate husband, and extremely kind and anxious father…Do, my dear sister, take good care of the dear portrait as it is all the likeness we have and someday Frances will value it highly. She mourns her dear father. She was his idol and she is his perfect resemblance, none of me or my family. I commend her to Your tender love and affection." Though she clearly mourned the loss of her husband, Betsey was fortunate enough to find love again, marrying William Swetland in 1829. Her letters to William show a great deal of affection, as well.

Frances Delord, daughter of Henry and Betsey, seems to have made a similar love match. Writing to her fiancé, Henry Webb, she explained, "Dear Friend, Let me confide that it is really the first time I have ever written a gentleman. It will be the stamp of an inexperienced hand. I would that the girl of your choice were more as she should be. The day you left here I felt quite lonely and deserted." An 1832 letter from Henry to Frances shows a similar devotion: "My Betrothed, It is with heartfelt pleasure that I take my pen to write you. Hour after hour has passed since we said goodbye. You cannot doubt that I feel anxious for the day that will unite us. You have my whole heart & if I have secured yours there is every prospect of our happiness. I estimate more & more highly your character & wish that I was more worthy of your love and esteem." Once married, Henry and Frances traveled through Europe on their honeymoon. Frances's journal details a trip to the Sistine Chapel and walking tours through the various cities they visited.

Some twenty-four years later, their daughter, Frances (Fanny), kept a journal of her own honeymoon trip to Europe. Having married Francis "Frank" Hall on May 14, 1856, Fanny remarked on the design and furnishings of railroad cars and rooms, the fashions of the women seen and the number and quality of dishes served at mealtimes. Fanny's letters to her husband mix expressions of love with discussions of the duties to

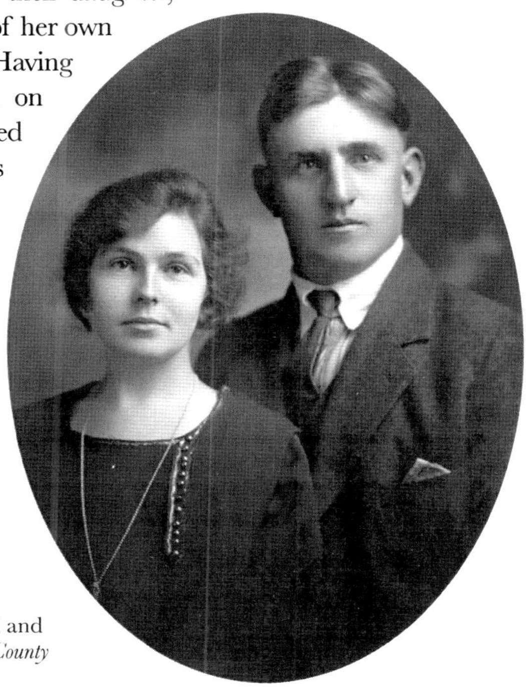

Mattie Cheeseman and her husband, Marshall. The Ellenburg couple lived and worked on their family farm. *Clinton County Historian's Office.*

which they both were called. After Francis volunteered to serve as a chaplain in the Civil War, Fanny wrote, "My dearest one, Do you know the depth of your own wifey's love? I feel that you did right in going last night for I feel, and so do you, that duty called you to go. We love each other too much & our many years of married life have bound us together too closely not to have it a real trial to have you go on this new duty. The telegram from Washington came to me last evening and what a relief & comfort it was…Thursday. Your precious letter from W. came home this noon. It does truly seem you are called to this chaplaincy. God bless & keep you. Fannie Fair." Other, later letters describe Fanny's work with the Women's Relief Corps and Women's Christian Temperance Union and Frank's work as a chaplain and minister in Plattsburgh, but all show a playful though clearly abiding love between the two.

Pliny Moore and his wife, Martha Corbin Moore, who married in January 1787, are described as having had a happy life together. Of Martha, Allan Everest wrote, "She was a remarkable woman, a classic example of a model helpmeet [*sic*] to a pioneering husband. Yet in keeping with the times, it was a male-dominated household, for Pliny made the decisions and firmly laid down the law."

Becoming a Mother and Creating a Family

Motherhood seemed to be the next step on the journey through life, though many women—like Fanny Hall—never became mothers. For those who did, the experience was varied. Dr. David Kellogg relates the story of a woman who had given birth to nine children before he attended her and, at the tenth confinement, proclaimed, "She should name her baby 'Enough.'" Louella North Kemble, daughter of the famed Children's Court judge, recalls, "Neither of our parents had the kind of daily responsibility of child care that I have had with mine. They ate alone, as Tom and I were fed at a little table in the den. Mother did a great job as executive in running the establishment and employing qualified help, but she knew very little about cooking or housekeeping itself." Yet, other stories of motherhood recall great care for one's children. Miss Mary Miner, in *Reminscences of Old Chazy*, for example, wrote, "One of the customs related to me, when I was very young and which excited my interest, was the mode of riding on horseback, when a woman would place one child in front of her on the horse, and hold another in her arms."

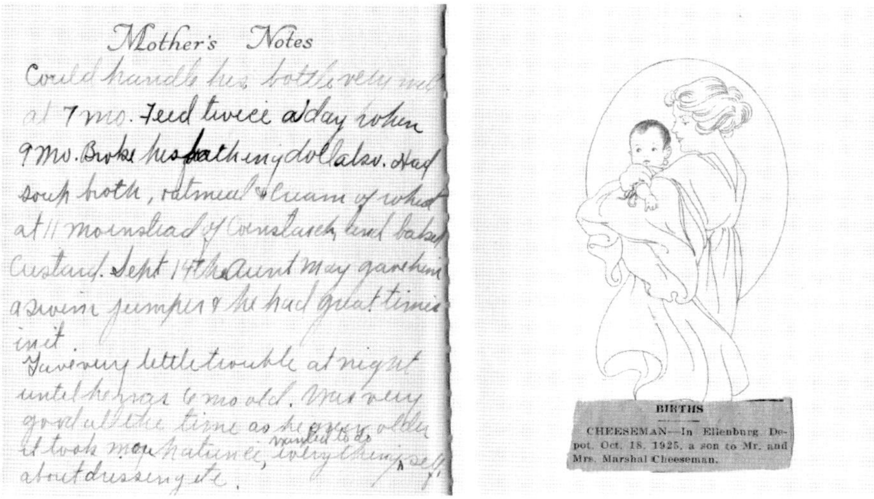

Mattie Cheeseman maintained two baby books detailing her much-loved son's growth. *Clinton County Historian's Office.*

Betsey Delord seemed to revel in motherhood. In 1823, she wrote to Frances, "My dearly beloved child, your mother cannot express to you how happy I was to receive a letter from her Daughter. To know that you was [*sic*] in health quite cheered me. I was dressing for Mrs. Addoms party when your letter came, but I sat down, read and wept over it. Grateful to god that he had preserved my child. Continue, my love, to offer your infant Prayers for your Mother and that you may safely be restored to her. Be kind to your dear father. You must be lonesome. Cheer each other." Then, in 1829, she expands on a similar theme: "My too dear daughter, Your mother chooses this time after her daily labor is over and before your father [William Swetland] comes home for tea to write and tell you how lonely and desolate I have felt without you. I was so anxious how you got over the bad roads that when your father came to tea and brought Mr. B. with him and he told me he met you near Chazy, I was much relieved."

For some mothers, the journey into motherhood brought great sadness. Certainly Betsey Delord experienced a tremendous loss when her daughter, Frances Webb, died in 1834 after contracting an infection during childbirth. Frances was excited to become a mother, writing to her husband in October 1833, "My Beloved Husband, Happy was I to know that the idea of becoming a father is pleasing to my husband. What a new train of feeling does it introduce and awakens in me an interest that seems to bind you more closely to my heart." But she was also increasingly worried that she would not live to be a mother. That same letter to Henry continues, "If I am blessed to be a mother, may I be enabled to discharge fully those duties encumbent upon me"; in another moment, she wrote, "I endeavor and feel it my duty to keep up good courage. Still I cannot look forward to the event without having my fears as well as hopes."

The February 11 announcement of the birth of a daughter, Frances, (she "is safely delivered of a fine healthy daughter") was quickly followed by accounts of the difficult labor and increasing illness ("she has been very, very sick"). By March 9, 1834, Betsey wrote, "My dear husband, All hopes are given up for the recovery of our dear Frances. Night before last she thought she would live but a short time, called in Mr. Webb and told him her wishes as regards himself and child. She had previously made known to me her wishes and has been perfectly calm and resigned to God's will." Frances died on March 15, 1834. Of this loss of a mother, Margaret Davidson, the Plattsburgh poet, wrote a thirteen-verse tribute that ends "with thoughts of the motherless Frances": "But the spirit we mourn has ascended on high, / And there it will watch o'er its little one's fate; / In whispers her voice will be heard from the sky, / with a mother's affection which ne'er can abate."

Although Davidson's poem does not address the sense of loss experienced by mothers whose children have died, that sadness, too, is a significant part of the story of Clinton County's past. One group of mothers in particular can tell the story of loss and of commemoration, through their efforts to remember their fallen sons and daughters.

An organization known as the Gold Star Mothers was organized by Grace Darling Seibold after her son died in World War I. Realizing that, left unchecked, her grief would prove self-destructive, Grace "devoted her time and efforts to not only working in the hospital but extending the hand of friendship to other mothers whose sons had lost their lives in military service." That service led to the creation of a group "consisting solely of these special mothers, with the purpose of not only comforting each other, but giving loving care to hospitalized veterans confined in government hospitals from home." Named for the gold star hung in windows in honor of deceased veterans, the association was incorporated in 1929 and chartered by the Ninety-eighth Congress of the United States in 1984. Originally open only to mothers who had lost a child in the Great War, membership was later expanded to include mothers who had lost a child in World War II, the Korean War and the Vietnam Conflict. The group's charter objectives, according to the organization's website, are to:

Keep alive and develop the spirit that promoted world services; Maintain the ties of fellowship born of that service, and to assist and further all patriotic work; Inculcate a sense of individual obligation to the community, State, and Nation; Assist veterans of World War I, World War II, the Korean Conflict, Vietnam, and other strategic areas and their dependents in the presentation of claims to the Veterans' Administration, and to aid in any way in their power the men and women who served and died or were wounded or incapacitated during hostilities; Perpetuate the memory of those whose lives were sacrificed in our wars; Maintain true allegiance to

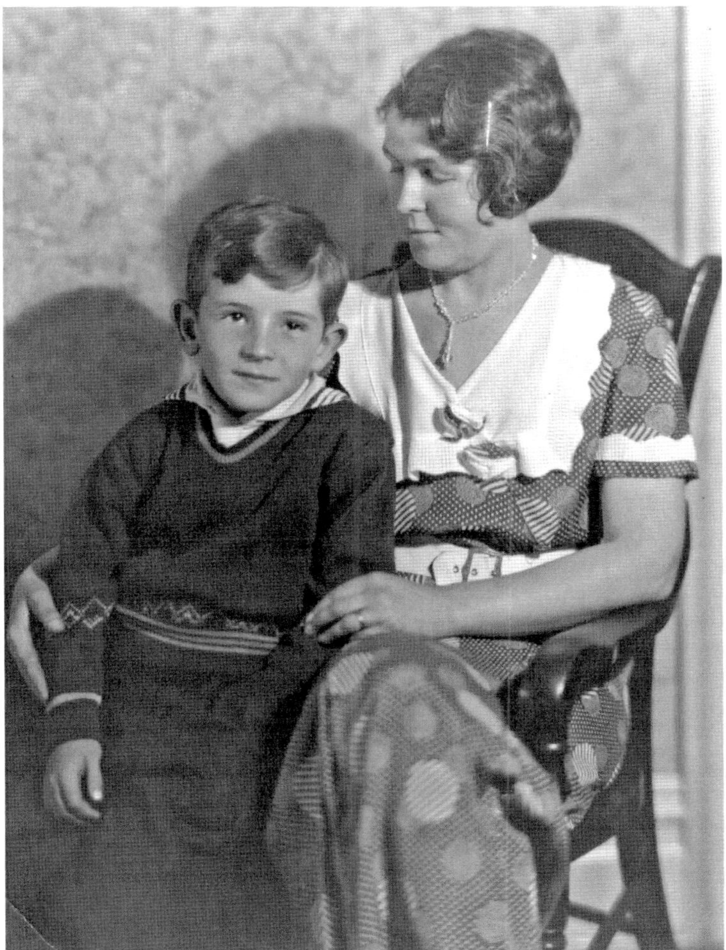

Mattie Cheeseman, with her son Winford. *Clinton County Historian's Office.*

> *the United States of America; Inculcate lessons of patriotism and love of country in the communities in which we live; Inspire respect for the Stars and Stripes in the youth of America; Extend needful assistance to all Gold Star Mothers and, when possible, to their descendants; to promote peace and good will for the United States and all other Nations.*

When, in 1929, the legislature appropriated money to support the pilgrimages of Gold Star mothers and the widows of soldiers, sailors or marines to the graves of World War veterans in France, England and Belgium, ten women from Clinton County qualified for the trip. Among them, Abbie Clukey, of 293 Margaret Street, Plattsburgh, lost her son George, buried in France, while Catherine Morgan's son Thomas and Elizabeth Peets's son Norman were lost in the war. Edward Lemieux, son of Matilda Lemieux, of 162 Cornelia Street, Plattsburgh; Edward Potter, son of Rose Potter; and Berton Chase, son of Cora Sanborn, of 45 Couch Street, Plattsburgh, were all killed in action and buried in France. Edith Blaney of Sciota; Ellen Manor of Altona; Minnie Mayo of 113 Lake Street, Rouses Point; Vina Morford of Route 1, Harkness; and Mary Davison, of Mooers Forks, also lost children in the war.

The individual stories of these women were not recorded by the local newspapers, though we do know that Abbie Clukey, Rose Potter and Minnie Mayo journeyed across the Atlantic Ocean to visit the graves of their sons. Prior to Mrs. Clukey's June 19, 1930 departure, a reception was held in Plattsburgh. At the ceremony, described in the June 20 *Plattsburgh Sentinel*, the Twenty-sixth Infantry band performed, the honor roll was read and various dignitaries from the community "paid tribute to the Gold Star Mothers in recognition of their courage, their devotion and their sacrifice that justice and right shall survive among the nations of the earth." One of the speakers, Harold Jerry, expressed his belief "that of all the battles fought the greatest battle has been fought in the hearts of the mothers of the boys who had given their lives in this great cause." During at least one ceremony held in France, President Gaston Doumergue said, "The love of all France goes out to the mothers who came to visit the land where their sons made the supreme sacrifice."

A pilgrimage like no other, this journey, or its possibility, connected mothers to the places of their children's deaths. A writer for the *Plattsburgh Sentinel* wrote eloquently of the option on April 18, 1930, "The Gold Star mother is at least given the comfort of knowing that her boy's grave has been cared for—that the grateful people for whose homes he fought and died have not neglected him. They may go and see for themselves, linger beside those precious mounds and know that all could be done is done." Even the mothers who chose not to make the journey were connected. Describing a mother who had not yet decided whether to accept the offer, a *Plattsburgh Daily Republican* writer, on May 9, 1930, said, "This mother seemed unusually quiet and unassuming, although there was a certain expression or look about her face that can hardly be described in words—an expression of pride that she too was a member of that legion of the 'Gold Star,' albeit an expression that somehow reflected the unspeakable grief that had been hers. She looked fondly at his photograph that hung on the wall. There was nothing boastful in her attitude. Indeed, her countenance was a kindly one, long resigned to what fate decreed and reluctant to talk about her boy."

Indeed, Clinton County's Gold Star Mothers did take pride in their children's service. On December 10, 1950, a war memorial was dedicated in memory of those who died in the two world wars. The marker initially included the names of 270 Clinton County war dead, though the names of those who died in Korea and Vietnam were added later thanks to the efforts of mothers like Bernice Conley, whose son Michael died in Vietnam. Above the names of the war dead is the inscription that forever ties these mothers to their children: "Erected by the Clinton County Gold Star Mothers in memory of their sons who made the supreme sacrifice in World Wars I and II."

BLENDED FAMILIES

When the death was of a spouse instead of a child, innumerable Clinton County families had to adjust to life with only one parent. Many families continued on in that fashion, with the surviving parent doing the work of mother and father. Others, though, remarried and created blended families. That tendency, to recouple and combine the children of previous marriages, is not new. In fact, Peter Sailly, after the death of his first wife, married Marianne Grellier in 1789. Grellier had come to Plattsburgh with the Sailly family. So, too, did Dr. Oliver Davidson, father of the poets Margaret and Lucretia, who married Miss Miller after his first wife's death, and Judge Caleb Nichols, who married the sister of Josey Green after his first wife—the widow of Joseph Ketchum—had died.

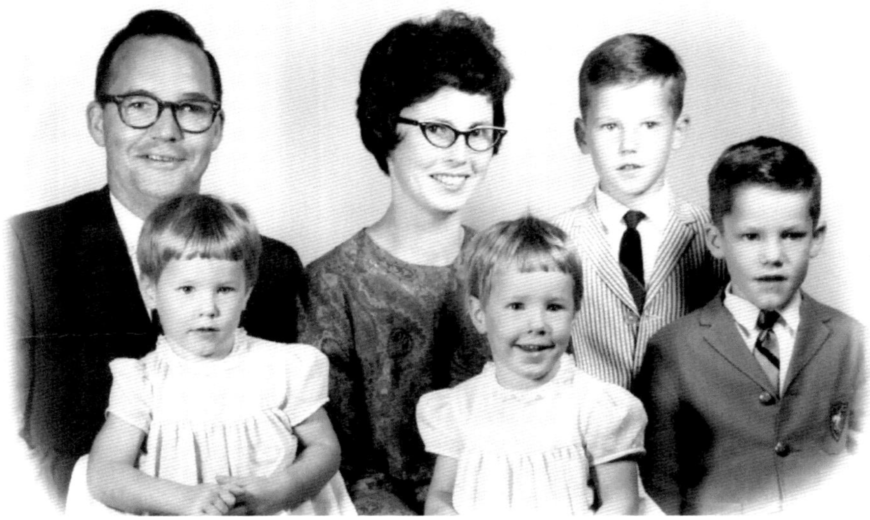

John and Patricia Roach, with their children, Kathleen, Eileen, John and Jimmy (left to right). *Kathleen Roach.*

John and Mary Roach represent another example. After a long illness, John's first wife, Patricia Roach, died on Tuesday, October 23, 1973, at the age of forty-one. A 1952 graduate of St. John's Academy and a 1954 graduate of the Plattsburgh State Teachers College, she taught at several schools, including the Northside School at Plattsburgh Air Force Base; she was also active at St. Augustine's Church in Peru, teaching religious education, participating in community affairs and charitable activities and serving on the parish council, the school board and the Home and School Club. At her death, she left her husband, John, as well as her children, John, James, Eileen and Kathleen.

Mary was raising her children on her own while working as a surgical nurse at the Champlain Valley Physicians Hospital. When the two met and married, they combined families in an admirable way, raising their children in a home that valued family, service to the community and faith. John's 2013 obituary sums up this family's story:

> *On July 5, 1980 John married Mary Elizabeth Woodward Keefe. They blended families as he became a much loved stepfather to Patrick, Kevin, Doreen, Danny, and Donna…John adored "his bride" as he called her and she adored "her boyfriend" as she called him. They spent 33 wonderful*

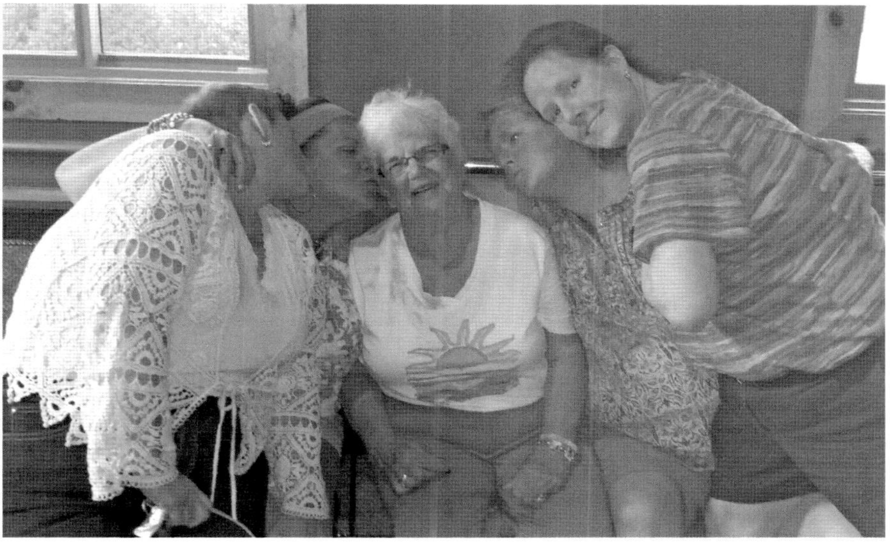

Mary Roach with her "girls": Donna, Doreen, Eileen and Kathleen (left to right). *Kathleen Roach.*

> *years together in true partnership built on respect and love. In their later years, they traveled to every corner of the U.S. in their RV. Mary was up for any adventure he could plan and was by his side until the end! Theirs was a love to be emulated.*

GRANDMOTHERS AND AUNTS

Of course, women did not have to be mothers in order to have strong family ties. Grandmothers and aunts—adopted or biological—have played an important role in the lives of Clinton County's children since the first settlement. Dr. Kellogg describes, for example, the birth of a poor woman's child, under cold and wet circumstances. Seeing the new mother's distress, her sister "took off her own stockings and put them on to the feet of the sick one, going stockingless herself and barefooted this morning." Marjorie Lansing Porter tells the story of another woman, Polly (Ketchum) Averill, known as "Aunt Polly," who "made a long-drawn out church service less uncomfortable for a little girl, Marian Packard, by wrapping her 'circular' around her, letting her hold a big muff against her cheeks and putting a foot stove close by."

One grandmother, Betsey Delord Swetland, had a particularly active role in raising her granddaughter, Fanny. Betsey took her granddaughter to raise, writing to her son-in-law:

> *I shall endeavor to have her brought up the same way as your sainted wife, both for you and myself. Thus far she promises all I could wish. After the nurse is gone and I have her more to myself I shall be able to train her mind as I wish. To this fact I in a great measure attribute all the loveliness of my dear child. Her mind like a piece of white paper was left entirely to be imprinted upon the direction of her Mother without having to contend with others' notions and in this respect I conceive it to be of importance that no association that might have a bad tendency should operate upon her.*

Eventually, Frances went back to live with her father, much to her grandmother's distress, and, after his death, lived with her aunts. One of those aunts, Eliza Webb, wrote a letter to Betsey, as dictated by Fanny, on July 12, 1838: "My beloved Grandmother, I thank you for your letter to your little Frances. I think of you & talk about you very often, and shall always love you. My aunts think me much changed since last summer. They say I am taller and thinner than I was then. They love me & wish me to be frolicsome & happy…I study my book a little each day & sew & run about in the garden & ride often over to Wethersfield to see my friends."

Betsey's constant wish for Fanny to be with her, despite her clearly happy surroundings, was evident in a birthday message written in 1952:

> *This day, my beloved child, is the anniversary of your birthday. It recalls many scenes both pleasant and painful. Well do I remember when you was* [sic] *handed into my arms by Doct. James. I took you wrapt* [sic] *in blankets and thanked God that your Mother was safely delivered of a living child. Little did I think that she, I so much loved, was so soon to be taken from me and you left a motherless child. But in my heart I adopted you as mine and for a short four years I was permitted to have the charge of you and often pressed you to my heart lest you might be taken from me. I never would have been willing to give you up had I been permitted to keep you until you arrived at womanhood. It cost me nearly as much to part with you as the loss of your mother. Little then did I think I should be spared to see your eighteenth birthday. I trust that now when you are nearly through with your school I shall be permitted to have you more with me…*

Emma Learned Kingsland, in *Old Keeseville Tales*, tells of another adopted aunt, Anna Woodman, describing her as a

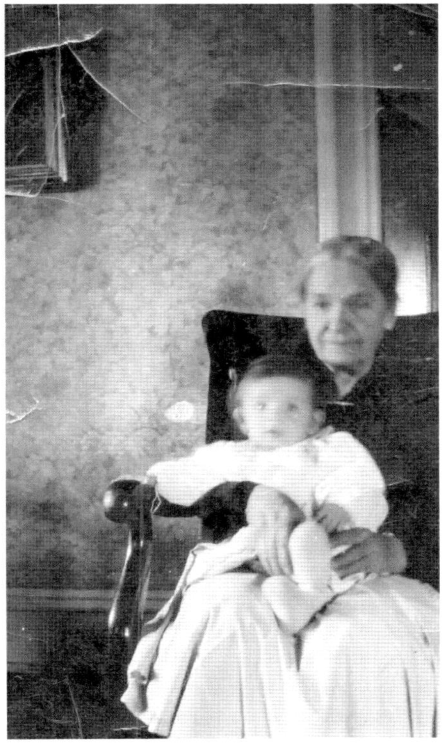

An unidentified woman, presumably a grandmother, rocking a young child. *Clinton County Historian's Office.*

> *friend of the children. Mary Ann Matthews, Anna Arthur, Julia and Nelly Mattocks, Julia Cowlbeck and I were her daily visitors, carrying in some little thing for her to eat; and in return she allowed us to rummage over her treasures, packed away in her bureau, and she would tell us stories of her early life, of her father, a prominent man and well-to-do physician, and how every year she went to Boston, bringing back to her New Hampshire home the fashions, as dear to the feminine heart then as today, and of her riding on horseback to "Hio," as she always called Ohio, and to Pennsylvania, and then, pathetically, of how she received attention from ministers and doctors and lawyers and here she was today an old maid and dependent on her friends for her daily bread. Dear old lady, I see her now, tall, slender, and dignified, still bearing traces of youthful beauty. We did not doubt in the least that she had been a beauty and a belle, and our hearts went out to her in sympathy. When she was ill we cared for her in her little house down near your railroad station, and were with her in her last days. Julia Cowlbeck was with her, I think, the night she died.*

Similarly, Eliza Carpenter, a milliner in Ellenburg Center, was known as "Aunt Eliza in the neighborhood. Those who knew her were impressed with the simplicity and purity of her life, her thoughts and her language as well as the saintliness of her character." Myra Magoon White describes her as "warm hearted, noble minded and decidedly pious. She was very talented in

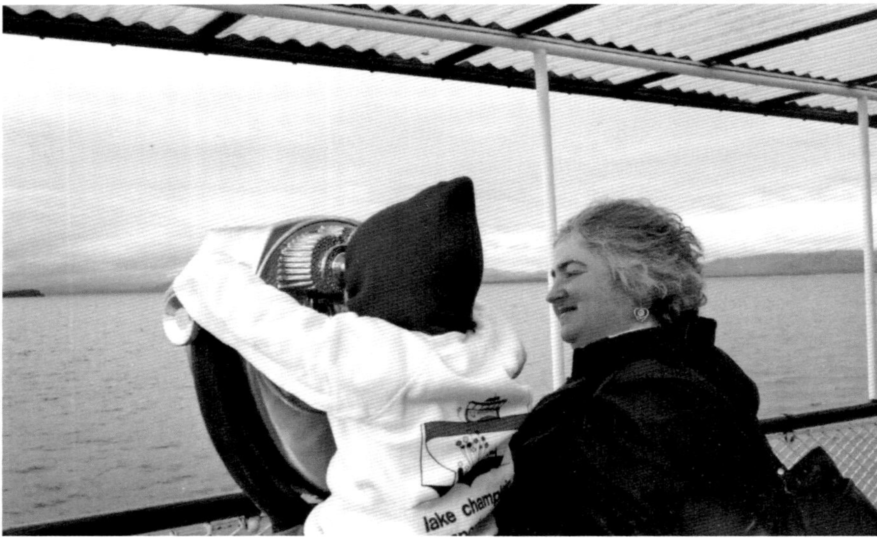

Gloria Pratt and her great-nephew Alex Lamont on Lake Champlain. *Author's collection.*

speaking and singing and was a member of the Methodist Episcopal Church choir for many ears. She was one of the few who died of old age, being over ninety years old at her death. She retained all her faculties, except hearing, to a remarkable degree almost to the day of her death."

THE LOVE CONTINUES

While not every familial relationship is one of love and respect, Clinton County clearly has had a high number of women who were held in the greatest esteem, during their lives and after their deaths. It seems important to note, then, that the love of individual women—women far too numerous to list in their entirety—continues, shown through family stories, photograph albums, home videos and even memorial tributes. Catherine Macomb, for example, is remembered as "a devoted partner, venturing with her husband to camp and garrison. In Plattsburgh, she witnessed the battle from the elevation west of town and wrote a poem about it. She was an intelligent, beautiful woman of elegant mind and manners, who made Macomb's home pleasant and hospitable." She was also the mother of twelve, nine of whom survived her when she died in childbirth in 1822.

Even when not survived by children, women were honored by their communities. Rebecca Laflin Leeke, who died at the age of ninety-three, was remembered in Dr. Kellogg's journals. Of her, Kellogg wrote, "Mrs. Leeke had taught school before 1815. She was married to David Leeke in 1820. He died in 1856, I believe, she having survived him 32 years, more than a single generation. Her children had all been dead for some years. Today a funeral procession winded its way to Pt. au Roche carrying the body there to moulder back to the dust of the earth. Indeed if it were not the hope of a future life the longest life here would be a matter of small moment."

Janet Duprey's tribute to her mother, Edna Calkins Lacy, is particularly poignant. Describing a mother who "became the 'woman of the house' at the age of 10 when her mother became ill," Duprey paints the picture of a woman who loved her family enormously. From her marriage of nearly sixty years (to Pete Lacy) to her clear pride in her children and their accomplishments, Lacy inspired her daughter, teaching her right from wrong, supporting her choices and loving her absolutely. Toward the end of her essay, Janet Duprey says, "Yes, my mother is my inspiration…throughout my Dad's illness and her own, she showed my family and me the true meaning of inspiration, dignity, courage and absolute love." Interestingly, Duprey has carried on that

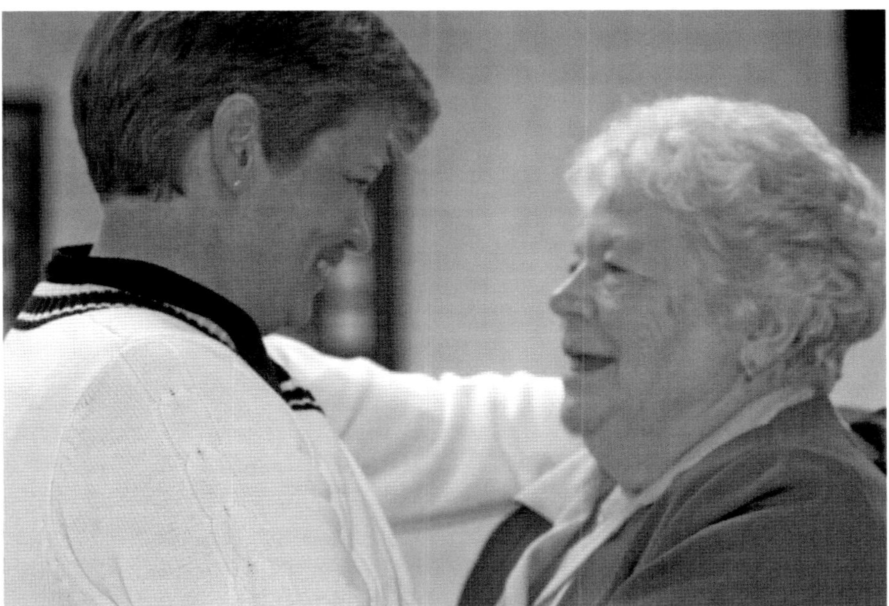

Cathy Phillips and her mother, Florence. *Author's collection.*

legacy through her actions as well as words, exemplifying the same traits for her children and grandchildren.

Another Peru family shows the power of a family's love. Florence Phillips, with her husband, Merton, raised two daughters and four sons in the town. Over the years, they watched their children excel at athletics and academics, start families of their own, open businesses and succeed in their careers. They also, sadly, experienced the loss of two sons before Merton passed away in 2006, after which Florence dealt with the further loss of her daughter Betty in 2013. Through all of those years, the Phillips family relied on the loving support of the youngest daughter, Cathy.

A physical education teacher and later athletic director at Peru Central School, Cathy was widely loved and respected. Her integrity and commitment to helping students achieve their very best, on and off the field, led to her election to the Peru Athletic Hall of Fame and various honors. Students at Peru have honored her by dedicating their yearbooks to her, but they have also honored her in less tangible ways. Learning from her actions, which always show a loving dedication to her family, countless students have come to value their own families because of Cathy, who even now—after retirement—participates in the life of the community and takes great care of her mother.

Chapter 2

WORKING

House and Farm Work

Much of the history of women in Clinton County centers on the home, which is a place of work as much as a place for rest, relaxation and family life. Part of that housework has long involved farm work. Tasks like feeding the chickens and slopping the pigs, planting and harvesting vegetables in a garden and gathering eggs have long been considered "women's work." Many of the jobs available to women outside of the home also involved housework, leading to a sense that housework is never done.

Nettie Senecal, who grew up in Ellenburg during the early 1900s, described in *Clinton County: I Remember When* the work she undertook, saying, "Housework was a chore. We had no electricity, no plumbing, no central heat. We didn't even have brooms. We had to make our own brooms by tying cedar branches to a stick. We had to make our own soap. We took ashes from a wood stove and put them into a barrel. We added a mixture of lye and water and to that concoction we added fat drawn from pigs we had butchered. We mixed this mess and let it set. Eventually it turned into soft soap." She continued to explain that, with this soap, "We did the wash by hand on a washboard. That left our knuckles raw, red and bleeding. Finally we bought a washer with a wheel. We put the clothes into the washer, filled the tub with hand-pumped water, and turned the wheel in order to swish the clothes around. We then had to tip the washer to empty it, refill the washer with clear water to rinse the clothes, tip the

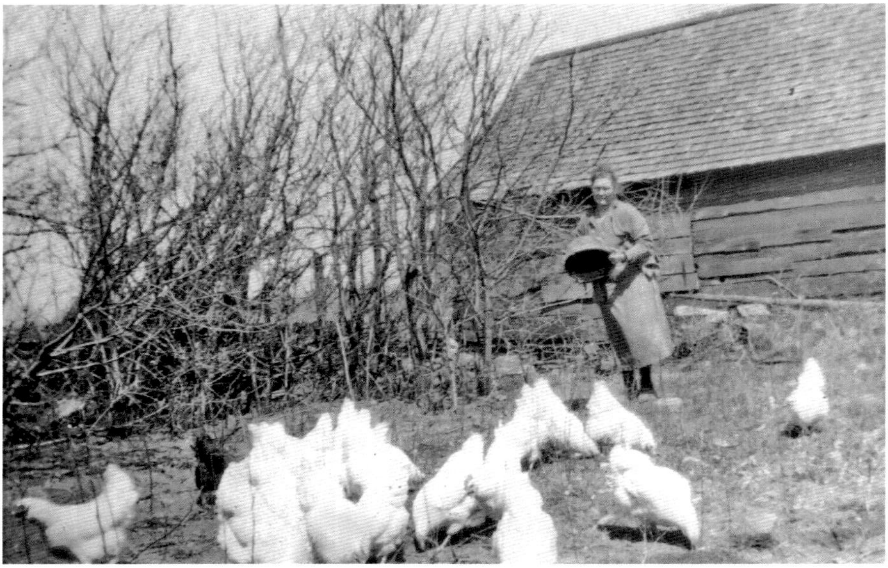

A woman feeding chickens on the Cheeseman farm in Ellenburg. *Clinton County Historian's Office.*

washer again to empty the water, and wring the clothes by hand. The clothes were hung on lines to dry."

Senecal further points out that her work included outdoor chores as well. She recalls, "Farm life was hard. I milked cows, dug potatoes, and pitched hay in big bunches onto the wagon. Since there was no machinery, everything was done with horses. I helped raise the sheep we had, sheared them, washed the wool, picked the dirt out of the wool, and carded the wool. I made clothes from the wool on a large spinning wheel with a shuttle at the top. In order to knit the clothes—stockings, underwear, socks, dresses, mittens, everything we wore—I had to walk endlessly back and forth working the shuttle."

For other women, farm work involved different tasks. Mabel Denton, of Peru, helped to sell the goods produced on her family's farm. In *History of Peru, New York*, she explains, "When I was a little girl one of my jobs was to take the milk to the butter factory with a horse and wagon to carry the large 200 pound cans, although they were not always full. At the factory, they had something that hooked onto the sides of the cans, lifted them up, and dumped the milk into a big vat. Then it ran out into the separator which sent the cream into one vat and the skim milk into cans which was taken back home to the pigs and calves. We were paid for the milk by the hundred pound."

Born in 1904 in Altona, Pearl Coryea explains that her family kept twelve milking cows, hogs, chickens and turkeys on their small farm. The animals were "all for food to feed us." Sugaring often added to the farm's holdings and supplemented the family's income. Yvonne Gonyo, who grew up in West Chazy and participated in Maggie Winans's oral history project, highlights the significance of that work, which involved four thousand taps a year on her family's farm. She describes the process:

> *To be assured of high grade syrup, much patience and watchful care was needed. The usual time for sap to run is mid-March, depending on the season. The middle of the season yields the sweetest sap. Each year the trees were tapped in a different place so as not to injure the tree and so the bark could grow back and heal the wound. Cleanliness was important as any bacteria spoils the sap. A pill was inserted into the hole, which was about three-eighths of an inch in diameter and one-half inch deep. The pill insured* [sic] *a long run, saved retapping, and also killed bacteria. The average yield was ten gallons of sap per year. Then the long round of collecting the sap began. The sap was poured in gathering tanks, then to a huge vat from which the sap was strained and flowed to the evaporator. It was automatically controlled by a float and held two hundred gallons. The machine was gravity fed, wood fired, using about forty-five cords of wood during the season. It takes about thirty-five gallons of sap to make one gallon of syrup. Much of this syrup was used to make maple sugar and maple cream.*

A 1932 graduate of the Plattsburgh Normal School, Alice Pardy Bubbins taught in various one-room schools for five years before beginning to work with her husband, William, on the CrossRoads farm in Beekmantown. The couple ran the farm, known by many as the "Alice Bubbins Farm," from 1936 until 1976. In addition to her farm work, Alice was a mother to a son and daughter, a grandmother to six and a great-grandmother to four. She worked with the Home Bureau and the Farm Bureau and served as the secretary of the Clinton County Industrial Development Agency from its beginning in 1969. Mrs. Bubbins shines as an example of a woman who was involved in both the daily life of the farm and the larger political and economic landscape of agriculture. A member of the Clinton County Farm Bureau Women's Committee, she was among a group of women who, in 1983, urged other women to get involved.

Marie Souza, chairman of that committee, explained in a February 15, 1983 *Press-Republican* article, "The future of agriculture is going to belong to those with

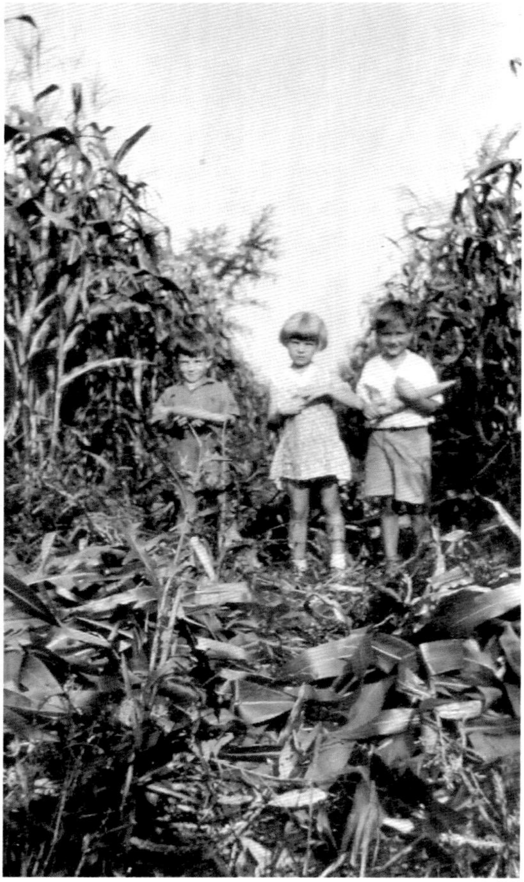

Children in a field, harvesting corn while playing. *Clinton County Historian's Office.*

a purpose and willingness to be involved." She said, "In 1919 the farmers banded together for a common cause because they felt the need for a strong agricultural program they had to look beyond their fences and they formed the Agricultural Farm Bureau Federation. In 1920 the need for women was realized because the permanency and dignity of agriculture, as well as the stability and happiness of country life, depends largely on the quality and strength of farm homes." Urging activism, especially insofar as it can help to improve the health and safety programs believed to stimulate patriotism, Souza, Bubbins, Carol Giroux, Alice Palmer, Bert Irwin and Rita Rae Laurin all offered a vision of farm women that moves beyond the normal jobs of the farm. Mary Lou Brunelle, the first female milk inspector in New York State, embodies part of that vision.

Fruits also played a significant role in the county's past, with a booming apple industry, for example. Many women have worked for local apple orchards, in a variety of positions. Included among them are Patricia Sheehan and Linda Facteau, who manage the bakery and the produce departments, respectively, at Rulfs Orchard in Peru; Debbie Everett, whose husband's grandfather started Everett's Orchards in Plattsburgh; and Nina Sullivan, who owns Banker's Orchard in Plattsburgh. Phyllis Silver, Linda Tripp, Viola Thompson, Rose Besaw, Florence Senecal, Margaret Erno, Dorothy Dermody, Isabell Fountain, Monica Laramie and Gladys

Brean, along with many other women, worked in other capacities at local apple orchards.

Another woman, Phoebe Coe Flagg, is remembered by Marjorie Lansing Porter for her farm work within the confines of the village of Plattsburgh. During the early nineteenth century, she planted an extensive orchard on her Margaret Street lot of more than two acres. Included within this orchard were seven kinds of plums. While the act of planting a garden was not unusual, the sheer size of this undertaking earned Flagg a place in the history books.

Vegetables and vegetable gardens most often fell under the purview of women. From planting to weeding, harvesting to cooking, women were involved in every step of a vegetable's path through their homes. They contributed to their family's welfare and economic viability by providing this sustenance. Some, like Pamela Torrance Sears, learned about gardens from their mothers and grandmothers, adding the further step of canning vegetables, preserving fruits and making jams and jellies to last throughout the year. Farm stands, like those owned by Viola Felio, Barbara Garrant, Irene McKinney and Grace Preston (with their husbands), generally offered these jams and jellies, as well as fruits, vegetables and flowers raised on the family's farm. Other women, like Bessie LaBarge, Bertha Gonyea, Betty Ranchor and Florence Pelkey, particularly enjoyed cooking, canning and gardening.

Often housework focused on the creation of other goods necessary for life. Mary Miner explains, "Stores were not as accessible as at the present time and goods were very dear. Women came to houses and wove material enough to supply the family for some time; blankets and bedspreads were also woven." In later years, women's groups were established as ways to learn more about the household arts. When she organized the Home Bureau in the town of Clinton in 1936, Rose Bohon and her group focused on sewing, upholstering, tailoring, refinishing furniture, cooking and nutrition. The Busy Bees, a later version of the group in Ellenburg, continued in the same vein, "promoting higher living standards for the home and community." Their purposes are "to become better homemakers, be more informed and useful citizens by promoting education, peace and better health to sponsor a craft program of interest to all participants." Later women, like Diana Murray, Beatrice McCooey and Sandra Stone, were noted for making clothes for their children.

Emma Rollo LaBarre, described in *Ellenburg Yesterday and Today*, shows how the two worlds—work and home—often collided. In 1916, Emma married Edward LaBarre and promptly moved to New Hampshire, where they worked on a chicken farm. When they returned to Ellenburg, they purchased a series of farms, moving from one to the next as they operated the dairy farms and made maple syrup each year. Along the way, Emma supplemented the family's income by making homemade doughnuts and selling them to restaurants in the village of Chateaugay. Once they moved back to Ellenburg Corners in 1934, Edward bought a little grocery store

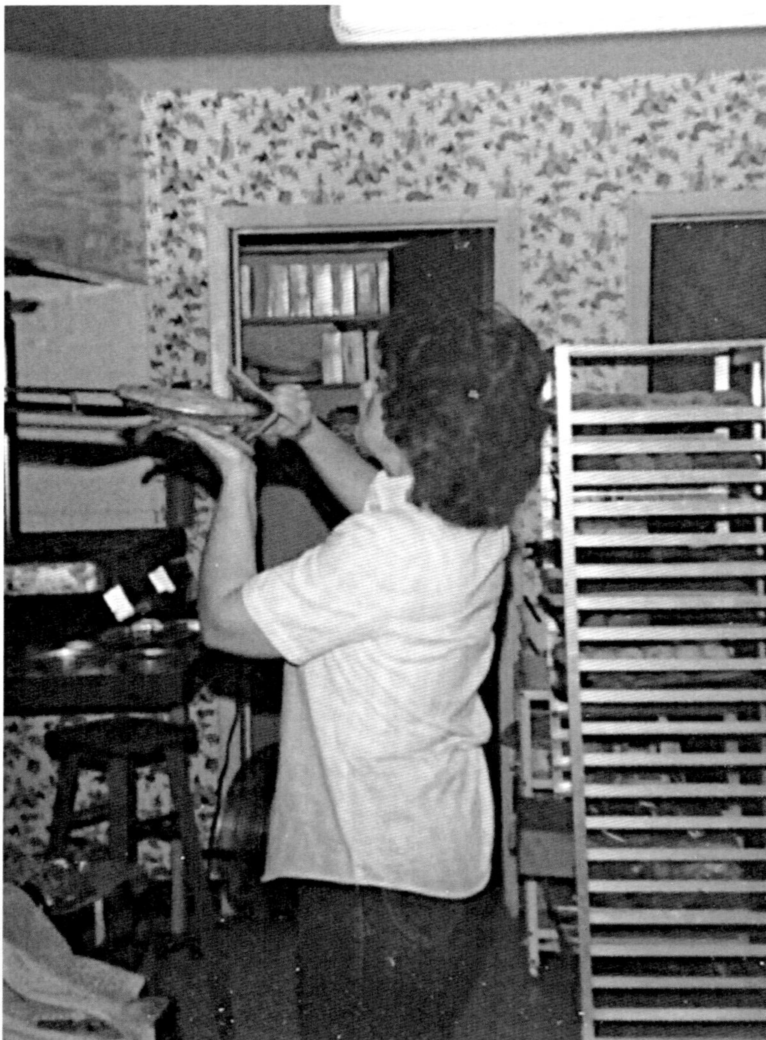

Mary LaMar taking a pie out of the oven of her restaurant, Green Acres Bakery, in Peru. *Christine LaMar.*

across the street, and Emma "opened an Ice Cream Parlor in a room of her residence where she lives at present…She served lunches and home-made doughnuts." Later, when the Ellenburg Central School was built, she took in roomers and boarders. By 1955, she had opened a small motel next to her house, running it herself until 1977. Beyond this work, LaBarre also raised eight children, and she, in turn, produced thirty-seven grandchildren and fifty-eight great-grandchildren. When Emma was ninety-two, she continued this housework, "getting her own meals and doing light housework."

For some women, housework constituted a paying job. Women throughout the county hired out, doing the work of the home for others. David Kellogg highlights several examples, including Mary Knowles, who left his employ to be married. Writing in 1886, Kellogg says, "She has lived with us since December 11, 1882. I have paid her in all $588, of which $6 was interest. She lost only 30 days' time and that was while her father was sick. She was a good, faithful woman in all respects and earned every cent of the wages I paid her."

Louella North also employed a woman to work within her house. Though North did all the cooking and cleaning after moving her family to Plattsburgh, Maggie Fauntleroy, according to North's daughter, "was a remarkable black woman who eventually became our full-time housekeeper after Mother became Children's Court Judge. Her dignity, competence, and loyalty are unforgettable, a wonderful model for young people who had previously had no association with anyone from a race different from their own." Others who did similar work, in private homes or in larger institutions, included Shirley Doner, Frances Stevenson, Evelyn Blow, Mae Ducharme Lavalley, Dorothy Smith, Elsie Rabideau, Ida Cayea, Betty Taylor, Beatrice Patten, Loretta Jiguere and Diane Macey.

FOOD AND LODGING

Even when not working in the homes of others, women have often worked in fields that build on the skills learned at home. Restaurants and hotels, in particular, utilize the same skill sets as housework. Among the women who have owned and worked in local restaurants are Mary LaMar, who was known for her excellent baked goods and sense of humor at the Green Acres Bakery in Peru; Doris Anderson, Julie Stevens and Angie Spiegel (the Homestead Restaurant in Plattsburgh and Chazy) and Debbie Helmer (Look What's Cooken in Plattsburgh), who cooked, waitressed and owned their restaurants, finding special coffee mugs for their regular customers; and Betty Rabideau, who owned the Chicken Delight in Rouses Point and reminded her customers that her peach shortcake was not good—it was great. Patty Waldron, Catherine Silver, Irene Rowe, Olive Duval, Ruby Gooddell, Becky Blaise Garrow and Elizabeth Van Etten have owned restaurants of one sort or another. Still others, like Betty Vann, Judy Sears, Maxine Ghrist, Barb Golden, Amy Gardner, Missy Stone, Terri Winterbottom and June Mott, waited tables, serving food as well as good will.

Other women who have worked in local restaurants, in every capacity—from owner to dishwasher—include Shirley Doner, Catherine Silver, Mary Deno, Ann Gamache, Eleanor Begore, Cora Supernaw, Leatrice Blaise, Dorothy Angelos, Rosemary Fedele, Michelle Barry Esposito, Natalie Turner Laundry, Elizabeth Doucette Deno, Anita Kefalos, M. Jane Compagnone, Marie Senecal, Bernice Belgarde, Laura Taylor, Electa Hislop, Mina Sherman, Margaret Rock, Patricia Barber, Irene Grigware, Beatrice Gadway, Shirley Sequin, Wilma Banker Murphy, Delia Gaillardetz, Merilda Shea Paul, Velina Adams, Carlene Belcher, Ethel Oliver, Mildred Carpenter, Kendra Murray Orton, Thelma Sorrell, Bertha Gordon, Lillian Bourdeau, Bertha Thompson, Marie Senecal, Marion Knox, Jeannine Pelkey, Lillian Bailey, Helen King, Evangeline Whalen, Leni Provost, Beatrice Brodi and Linda Darrah.

Women who have owned or operated bed-and-breakfasts, hotels, tourist cabins and campsites are Hannah O'Conner, Caroline Broadwell, Gertrude Patnode, Emma LaBarre, Rita Rae Laurin, Theresa Ouellette, Joyce Banker, Ellen Graves, Bernice Reardon, Nancy Freeland, Evelyn McGee, Gladys Lagoy and Monica Laverdure. Sarah Callahan, who worked at the Witherell Hotel, roomed at Miss Rooney's house, which she bought upon Rooney's death; when she retired, Callahan was given a watch that she valued so much she was buried with it.

One woman, recalled only as Miss Jennie L., ran "a den of ill-repute at Dannemora." In 1879, when three men engaged in a drunken brawl on her premises, she took out her gun and fired. The newspaper item, reprinted in Sarah Baker's *The Saranac Valley*, remarked, "We understand she intended the shot for another party, but Joseph's hand was in the way." Within the week she was "brought before Justice Jackson…for indulging too freely in the use of firearms, she having used a man for a target."

The production and consumption of alcohol created work for women in other ways, too. The Eighteenth Amendment to the U.S. Constitution, which went into effect in January 1920, prohibited "the manufacture, sale, or transportation of intoxicating liquors within, the importation thereof into, or the exportation thereof from the United States and all territory subject to the jurisdiction thereof for beverage purposes is hereby prohibited," while the National Prohibition Act, or Volstead Act, provided a means to enforce prohibition, with the intention "to prohibit intoxicating beverages, and to regulate the manufacture, production, use, and sale of high-proof spirits for other than beverage purposes, and to insure [*sic*] an ample supply of alcohol and promote its use in scientific research and in the development of fuel, dye, and other lawful industries." Given our proximity to the Canadian border, bootlegging was common, with women operating on both sides of the law until the Twenty-first Amendment repealed Prohibition in 1933.

Diane Filion helped to keep back roads open for use by smugglers until her car was seized when, she maintains, customs officers planted two bottles of whiskey in the car. "I decided not to make a legal case of it," Filion says, "If I won, my life would be intolerable afterwards."

According to Allan Everest in *Rum Across the Border*, female smugglers often concealed liquor on their bodies, making use of hot water bottles and other containers held under their clothes and even in their bloomers. In response to those trends, customs officers called upon their wives to help search women suspected of smuggling alcohol and, "during the heavy tourist season, Geraldine Laundree was appointed to the Rouses Point customs house by the collector of customs at Ogdensburg. In her three months of duty she removed 670 bottles of liquor from the persons of female tourists arriving from Canada and collected fines of $3,050. This was the first border port in the country where a woman inspector was on regular duty. So successful was the experiment that the practice was duplicated elsewhere, and Laundree herself was back at Rouses Point the next year."

While homebrew beer continued to be produced in barns, sheds and basements and customs agents patrolled the region looking for contraband, women throughout the region lived with the ramifications of Prohibition. Some reported shots fired, while others reported threatening behavior. Living in Champlain, near the Canadian border, Lavinia Bullis remembers "being so frightened one time that she crawled in the cellar window of her home" and, another time, witnessing a man hiding his liquor in their culvert before reporting to the Customs House. Another woman reported that a Rouses Point customs officer fired through the rear window of her car, missing her by inches, when he mistakenly believed her to be a bootlegger. On the southern side of the county, one woman married to a customs officer recalls the days of Prohibition as having been incredibly difficult. Beyond the ordinary concerns of women married to officers of the law, she had to deal with "anonymous letters threatening that she would never see him again if he didn't resign and naming a deadline."

LABOR UNIONS

Local women have also been actively involved in labor unions, fighting for the rights of the many through their association. One of the most active unions in the county is the New York State United Teachers (NYSUT), a union that is affiliated with the American Federation of Teachers, the National Education

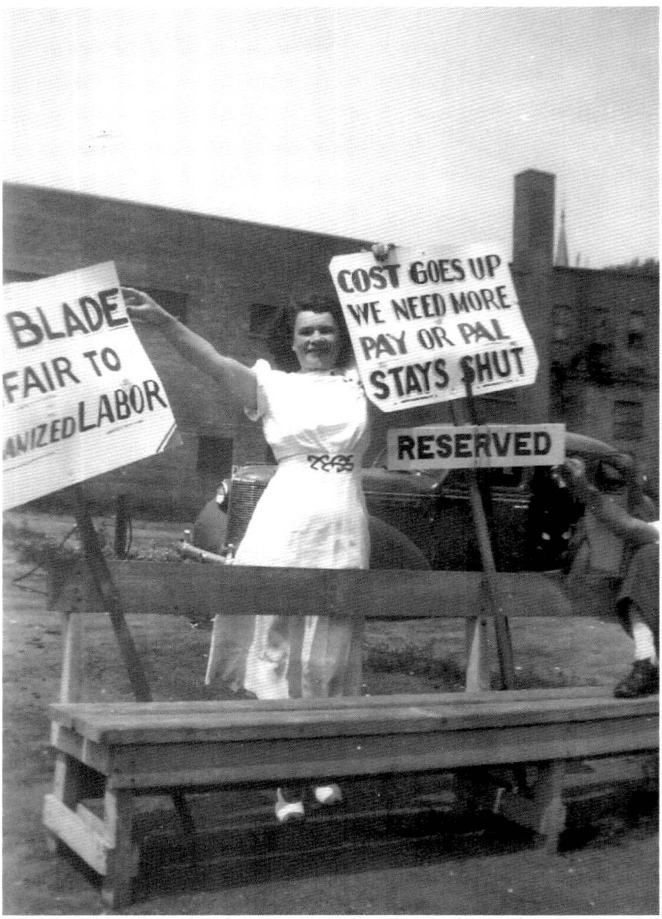

Ethel Forkey at the Pal Blade strike. *Clinton County Historian's Office.*

Association, the AFL-CIO and Education International. Locally, every school district has a teacher's union affiliated with NYSUT, whose members participate in rallies, conventions and actions in support of education. Kathleen Roach, a social studies teacher at Peru, and Tricia Sardella, an elementary school teacher in the same district, are especially active in the union, representing local teachers at national meetings and conventions.

Women were actively involved in the Pal Blade strikes of 1941, 1944, 1946 and 1950. In each instance, the union sought more equitable conditions, which ranged from the salary increases they believed "justified in view of the increasing cost of living and of increased production now being conducted at the plant," repayment of back wages and appropriate benefits. Included among the unions involved were Local 1585, International Association of Machinists, and Local No. 22,000, American Federation of Labor. Although newspaper accounts of the strikes do not refer to women involved in the action, photographs in the Clinton County Historian's Office show that women like Ethel Forkey were active members of the 1946 strike, walking the picket line with their colleagues. Pal Blade, which opened in 1935, made a variety of knives and razor blades, including some military-issue blades during World War II. The company was acquired by American Safety Razor in 1953, and the Plattsburgh facilities were closed in March 1954.

MILITARY SERVICE

Countless Clinton County women have served this region and this country through military and wartime service. Nancy Smith, for example, joined the Free French during World War II, serving in French North Africa and the Middle East, where she met her husband, LeClair Smith. After marrying him in 1941, she joined the U.S. Army and served in the Pacific Theater at Saipan and Iwo Jima. Later Smith served as the curator of the Kent-Delord House and co-founded the Tuesday Club.

Katherine Graham also served during World War II. A graduate of Plattsburgh High School who also attended the Plattsburgh Business Institute, Graham served as a liaison officer at the Third Marine Air Craft Wing in the U.S. Marine Corps Air Station at Cherry Point, North Carolina. She did parts inventory on Marine F4U fighter planes and remarked that "at one point, she assembled single-handedly enough parts to put together an entire fighter plane." Upon her return, she served as the chair of the first canvass for funds in the Plattsburgh Mother's Club Mother's March on Polio for the March of Dimes. The owner of a beauty salon on Broad Street, Katherine also worked in the Office of Senior Services in the Outreach Program and with the Retired Senior Volunteer Program at Clinton Community College until the early 1990s. She was a member of the Altar Rosary Society, the Altar Boys Mothers of St. John's, the Cub Scouts and the Boy Scouts.

Evelyn Lagree Watson also served her country through military service. "When World War II broke out," Watson's daughter Geri Favreau writes, "Evelyn enlisted in the Army Nurse Corps in November 1942 for the duration of the war. She enlisted at the Plattsburgh Barracks in Plattsburgh, NY. She entered into active duty on 14 January 1943 as a 2nd Lieutenant when she boarded a train in Plattsburgh headed to Fort Bliss Station Hospital in El Paso, Texas where she served 30 months. She served in the Army Nurse Corp for 3 years." During her time in the corp, Watson was also assigned to the Glennan General Hospital in Okmulgee, Oklahoma, which treated prisoners of war and included some captured enemy medical personnel as staff members. At the time of her honorable discharge on January 30, 1946, Evelyn was a first lieutenant who had been awarded the American Theatre Ribbon World War II Victory Medal.

After her discharge, Watson returned to Churubusco, with her daughter, to live with her parents. She served as a home nurse until 1950, when she became the school nurse teacher at Ellenburg Central School (later Northern Adirondack Central School), a position from which she retired in 1977. Although she had trained as a nurse at the Champlain Valley Hospital School for Nurses, graduating in 1941, Evelyn took night and summer courses for ten years in order to earn her bachelor's degree. Of this post-military life, her daughter writes:

> *Evelyn was always very involved in her community. She was the first "Rescue/EMT" in Busco many times being called on to treat injuries, give shots and minster to the sick. In 1991, she received the Living Treasures award from the Clinton County Office of the aging. She served as the Town of Clinton Historian; secretary of the Cemetery Association and treasurer of Churubusco Senior Citizens Housing Corporation and as a member of the Town Council for one year. She was a member of the Home Bureau, the Retired Senior Volunteer Program, Advisory Board for the Office for the Aging, Retired New York State Teachers Association, and American Legion in Chateaugay, NY. As a member of RSVP she took blood pressures, helped elderly citizens with*

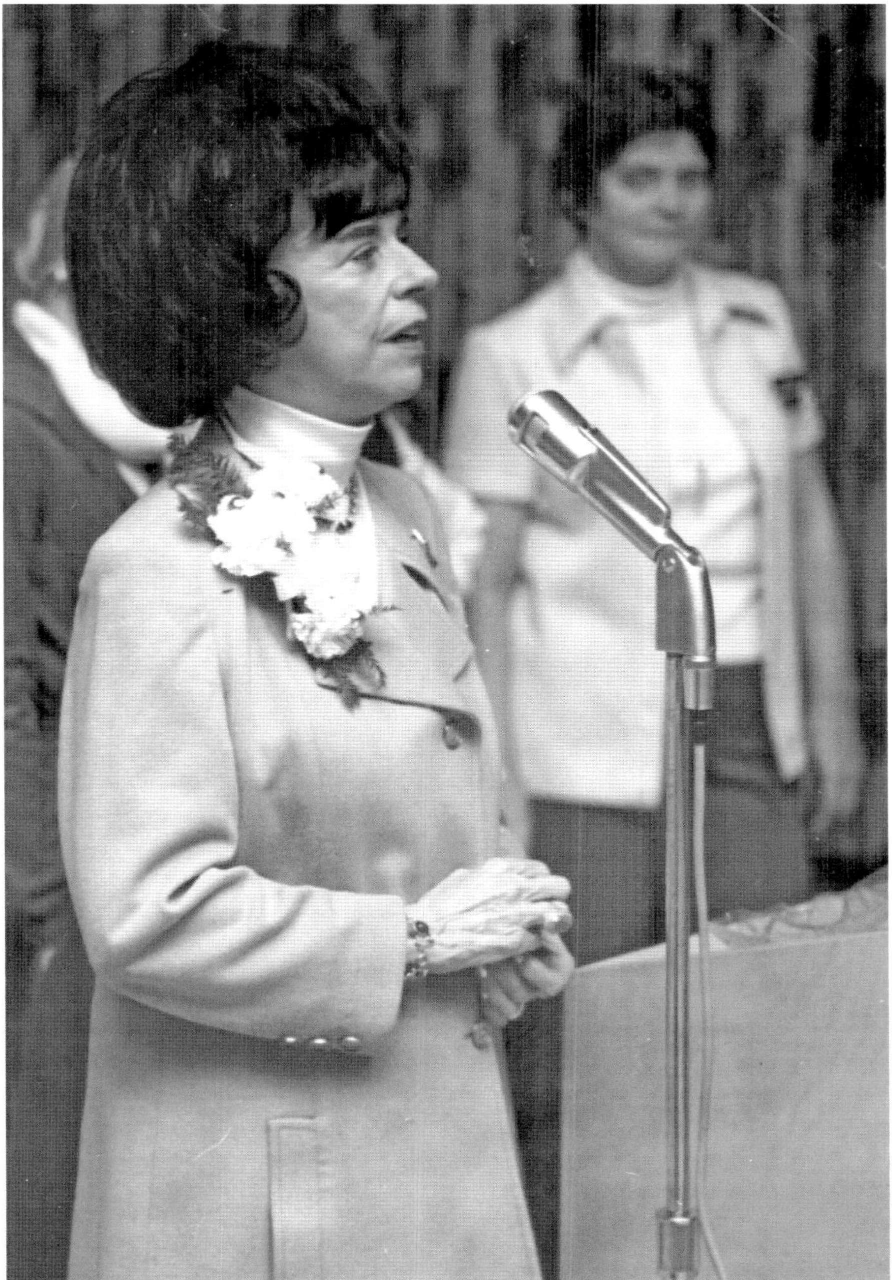

A visiting dignitary, addressing a group at the Plattsburgh Air Force Base. *Clinton County Historian's Office.*

> *their banking and was on call for senior's emergencies in the community. As a village resident she worked with others to form a Neighborhood Watch, was instrumental in getting free long distance to Plattsburgh, securing Lifeline service, and bringing Senior Housing to the community.*

Ethel Dick, in *Sacred Remembrances*, told the story of her husband, Myron Gracian Dick, a Korean War POW who died in captivity. She wrote, "We lived at a motel that rented apartments to military, and that's where we stayed until we got a place on base, a little apartment. I got pregnant while I was there and had a baby girl, Catherine. When my little girl was a year old, on July 25, 1950, the day before her first birthday, Myron left for Korea. They went to the ship by Greyhound Bus and drove right by the motel where we were living. I was out there with the baby, so he could wave goodbye. That was the last time I saw Myron. He said, 'I'll be back in no time. We'll lick those guys.' He was wrong." Soon after Myron went missing in action, Ethel and her daughter were packed up to move back across the country to Clinton County. She has purchased a grave in Chazy, at the Ingraham cemetery, for her husband's remains, when they are returned to her.

Kathy Baumgarten, who joined the Women's Air Force in 1975 from Niagara Falls but has lived in Plattsburgh for some twenty years, explains that life was not the same for women in the military. "When I came in," she writes, "women didn't wear green and they did not wear battle dress uniforms. Not long afterwards, jobs started opening up for women. My job was in civil engineering, and I worked in the Entomology Section. I was the first enlisted woman to do that job on the base and only the second woman on the base to wear a green uniform. This isolated me socially from all the other women." After serving for eight and a half years, Baumgarten left the service to raise her family. Later, when her husband retired in 1993, she joined the Air National Guard out of Burlington, Vermont, to complete her twenty years. During that posting, she was in the 158th Fighter Wing and, with it, sent to Kuwait for Desert Storm. Now retired, Kathy continues her service to her country and to other military personnel, working with the American Military Retirees Association in Plattsburgh and with other veterans groups in the region.

Other local women who served during World War II, in roles as different as factory production and enlistment in the Women's Air Force, include Josephine Willis (Pentagon), Phyllis Silver, Helen Thoma, Mildred Hofbauer (Curtis-Wright Corporation Defense Plant), Anita Hall (U.S. Army), Alberta Smith (defense plant), Harriet Call (U.S. Army Air Corps' Women's Air

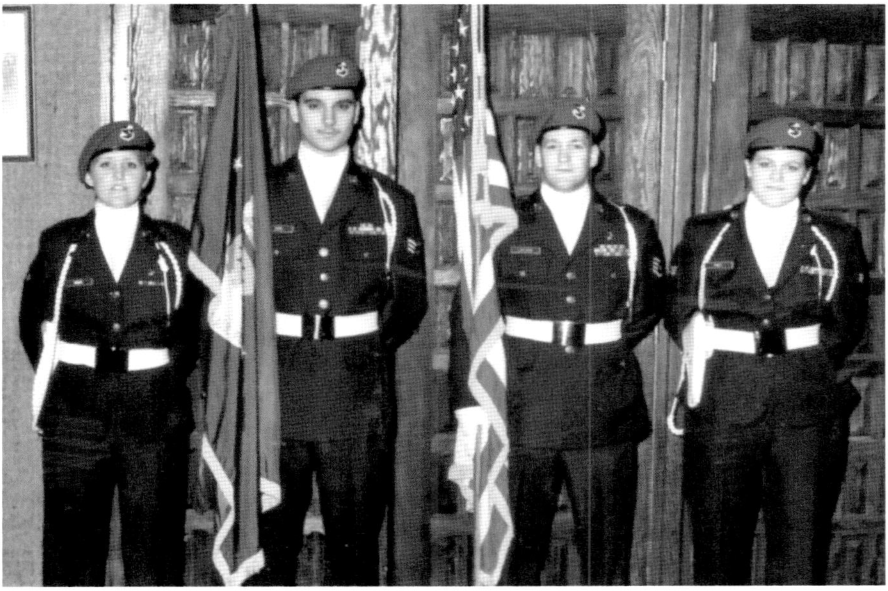

Plattsburgh Air Force Color Guard, circa 1985. *Clinton County Historian's Office.*

Force), Rita Duquette (U.S. Army nurse), Alma Swartz (Army/Navy Nurse Corps), Evelyn McMillan (U.S. Army), Mildred Collins (U.S. Army Air Corps), Agnes Durkee (airplane spotter), Mary Brady, Doris Gagnier, Evelyn McMillan (U.S. Army), Carita Mitchell, Rita Porter, Bernadette Primeau, Luella Recore, Barbara Hale (Red Cross), Pearl Lawrence (General Electric), Ruth Rivet (Red Cross), Jeannette Stohn (U.S. Army combat nurse), M. Anita Quinlan (Red Cross), Kathleen Clodgo (U.S. Army), Bernadette Lavigne (Savage Arms), Clara LaFrance (Alcoa Aluminum), Marie Andres (Chrysler Corporation, working on the B-24 Liberator Bomber), Bernadette Kinn Stockunas (nurse) and Gertrude Jarvis (Coast Guard).

Women who undertook service in the armed forces after the end of World War II include Anita Kefalos (Women's Air Force), Lillian Stelfox (teletypist for the Department of Defense), Madeleine Millett (U.S. Foreign Service), Maria Woitazek (USAF), Pamela Pooper McCarrier, Marie Peterson, Kathryn Delorme Jarvis, Pauline Bernard, Geraldine Vanderbeck, Kari Baldwin, Kathy Baumgarten, Anne-Marie Farrell, Nita Deyo and Robin Caudell.

From the wives of enlisted personnel and officers to the women who worked in civilian positions on the air force base, women have also served the military in a variety of capacities. One of the most noted of these women was Lois

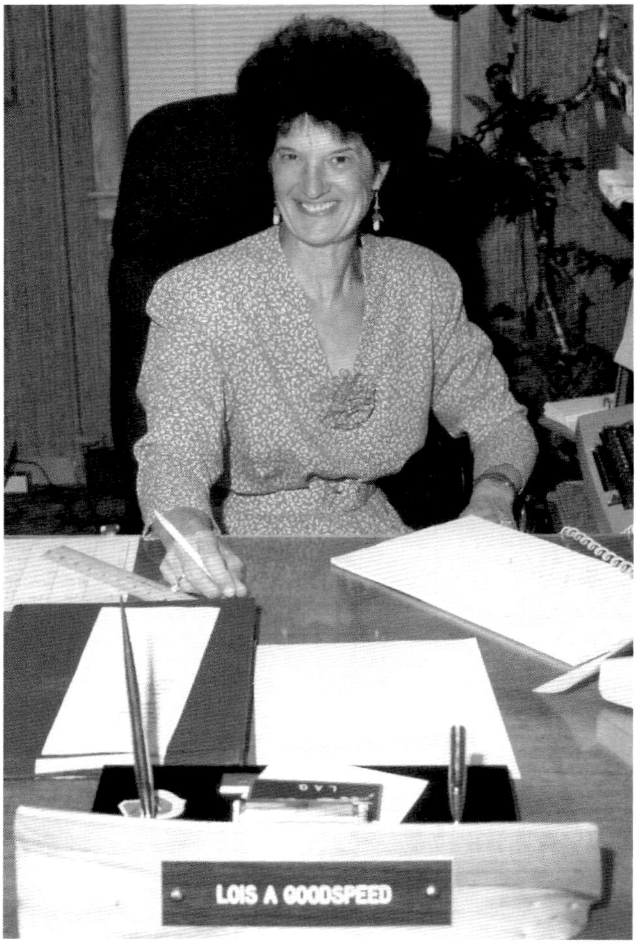

Lois Goodspeed at her desk in the Wing Commander's Office.
Clinton County Historian's Office.

Goodspeed, who retired as the secretary to the commander of the 380th Bombardment Wing, a Strategic Air Command facility, in June 1991. Before becoming a mother and focusing her efforts on her home, Goodspeed worked at Griffiss Air Force Base in Rome, New York, and she returned to that secretarial work during postings at Loring and Columbus AFB. In August 1961, Lois and her family moved to Plattsburgh Air Force Base (PAFB). She "started her first civil service job at Plattsburgh AFB when she was hired in April 1963 by the 820th Air Division Commander to become his executive secretary. Upon the inactivation of the air division in June 1965, she became the secretary to the wing commander. She has held that position ever since." During her time at PAFB, Lois worked for two air division commanders and seventeen wing commanders and witnessed a great many milestone events on the base. For example, Lois saw the last KC-97 departure and the arrival of the first KC-135A; she witnessed the deactivation of the 556th Strategic Missile Squadron and the awarding of the Fairchild Trophy in 1976, 1977, 1978 and 1984. She won several awards for outstanding service and was touted as being "the most valuable Base employee and the real bridge between Base and the community, the community and the Base and the super accomplishments of the 380th." Even after retiring, Goodspeed continued as one of the assistant secretaries for the Plattsburgh Air Base Liaison Committee.

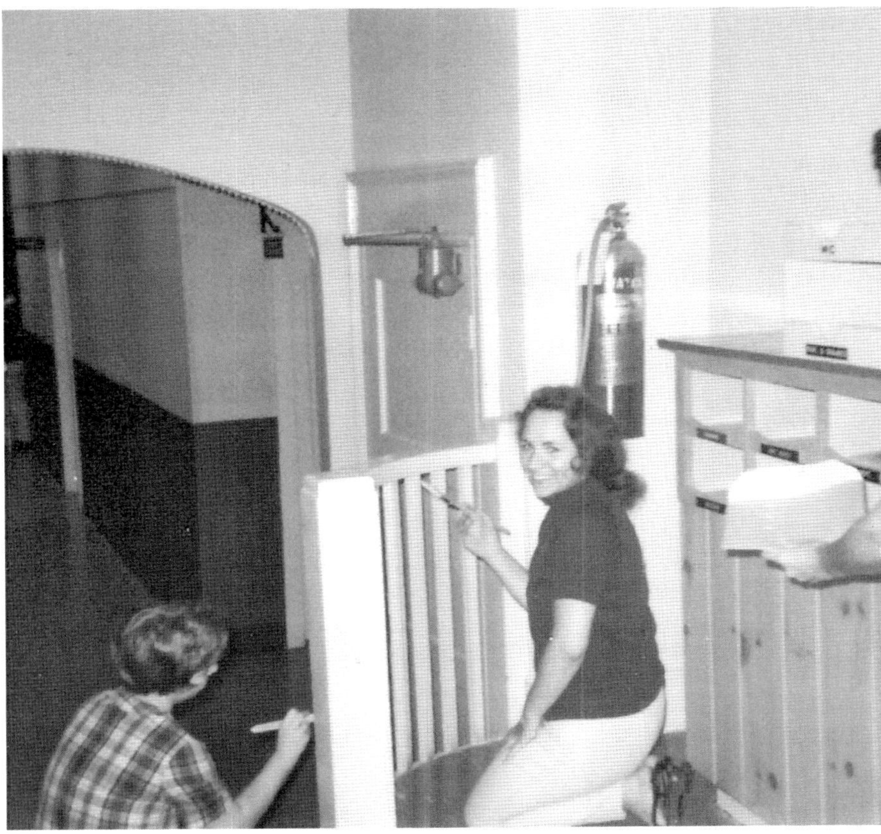

Barb Smith (left) and Janice Shannon painting outside Colonel Gunn's office in preparation for a base-wide inspection, circa 1968. *Paul A. Shannon.*

Other civilian jobs on base ranged from secretarial support to civil engineering, housekeeping to working in the commissary. Janice Shannon represents one group of these workers. A native of Chateaugay, Janice graduated from Our Lady of Victory Secretarial School in 1965 and began working at the Plattsburgh Air Force Base. While at the base, she met Paul Shannon, married and started a family. Though the Shannons were posted at various locations, including England, Texas and Nebraska, during Paul's twenty years in the air force, they were reassigned to PAFB in 1979, "a happy day since she was back home." During her years as an air force wife, Janice made many good friends, with whom she kept in touch. She is perhaps most remembered, though, as a stay-at-home mom, who "devoted her time and energy to raising…three children, Paul, Daniel, and Amanda. She was a regular at the kids' class functions and was the favorite chaperone on school trips."

Other women who worked on the Plattsburgh Air Force Base in civilian positions include Josephine Willis (Base Housing Officer), Patricia Landin, Susan Smith (a secretary at the PAFB hospital), Dorothy Angelos (a cook), Mary Recore (comptroller's office and wing commander's secretary, among other roles), Shirley Meader (General Dynamics at PAFB), Jeannette Schroeder (a cryptographer and then clerical worker at the PAFB credit union), Mary Gioiosa (honorary wing commander), Veronica Runyan, Geraldine Orlando (PAFB Exchange), Gloria Smith and Judy O'Brien. They are joined by the many women who have worked in support of active duty military and veterans, through their roles as wives, mothers and interested citizens. Included among the ranks are Eileen Ward, Pam Turner Ballantine, Jutta Purtell, Peggy Bureta, Emma Delucas, Marisa Pers, Mary Somody, Marion Moore Miner, Winifred Petrashune, Irene Latour, Iris Roe, Maria Arce and Jeanne Filion, who, according to a January 13, 1999 *Press-Republican* article, "knitted lap robes for veterans, collected stamps for the veterans rehabilitation clinic and raised Christmas money (and stuffed animals) for the army nurse and seven veterans on her floor" after entering the CVPH Skilled Nursing Unit.

Angela Bryant Forrence also served admirably. She was particularly concerned with soldiers who were prisoners of war or missing in action (POW-MIAs) and organized an annual POW-MIA remembrance day, a tradition that Mary Somody continued after Forrence's 2005 death. Steve Bowman, the director of the Clinton County Veterans' Services Agency, described Angela as someone who traveled the country to raise awareness about POW-MIA issues and as "very passionate about POW-MIAs and remembering (them) and trying to work toward bringing more of them home."

BUSINESS AND INDUSTRY

While factory work for women increased during World War II, when women often took up positions previously held by men, Clinton County's women have been employed by factories for more than one hundred years. After the end of World War II, that work continued in a variety of industries. Lovella Papin and Marjorie Brown were the first two employees hired to work at Ayerst Labs. Peg Barcomb writes, "Both ladies went to Montreal to learn finishing techniques. Marjorie Brown resigned shortly after and Lovella was the only female for awhile." They were later joined by many women, as the company shifted to Wyeth Ayerst and then Pfizer. Among the women

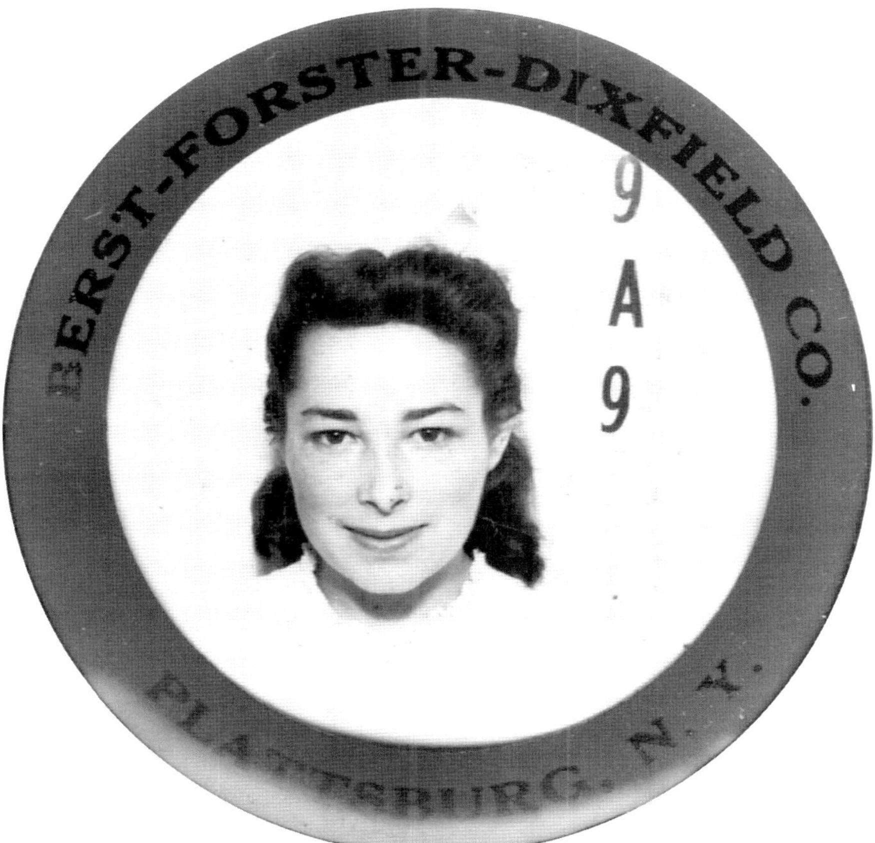

Doris Brown Trudeau's identification pin for the Berst-Forster-Dixfield Company and the Diamond Match Company. *Clinton County Historian's Office.*

who worked at the facility were Mildred Cororan, Irma Anderson, Julie Martineau, Christine Torrance, Jane Rabideau Forkey, Lois Doyle, Tracey McGivney, Norma Vassar, Barbara Criss, Natalie Aldous, Christa Covel Reyell and Margaret Shaner.

Making matches as well as containers for food, deluxe paper plates and paper sticks for lollipops, Diamond Match Company hired a significant number of women. One of them, Doris Brown Trudeau, donated a collection of memorabilia and histories to the Clinton County Historian's Office in 2008. Her materials, which include the company phone list, the funeral cards of company employees, correspondence from her former co-workers, timelines and photographs, indicate that Diamond purchased the Plattsburgh factory from Berst-Forester-Dixfield in 1944, selling a significant portion of the land and facilities to Vanity Fare, which was later sold to Georgia-Pacific. Women who worked at Diamond Match include Bette Brown McGowan, Priscilla Garrand, Doris Dashnaw Penn, Doris Hover, Catherine Smith, Pat McDonald Burgess, Marge Reeves, Ruth Smith, Olive Van Tassel, Mandy O'Neil, May Dranly Hopper, Verla Roby, Elsie Smith, Beatrice Rushford, Helene Frederick, Dorothy LaMora, Rosanna Hebert, Theresa Brault, Beverly Cleland, Lillian "Topsy" Couture, Gertrude Fifield, Thelma Corron, Mary St. John, Mildred Hofbauer, Della Marie Sample and Lina Lawliss Kelley.

Other women who worked within local factories, ranging from Georgia-Pacific and its predecessor Vanity Fare to Delegar, included Elsie Hart, Alice Ethier, Harriet Favreau, Barbara O'Brien, Grace Bruso, Evangeline Whalen, Theoda Lambert, Mildred Fayette, Gertrude Fifield, Rita Jennette, Viola Gold, Elnora Blaise, Julie Renadette, Ruth Cora Beardsley, Gladys Desso, Wilma Barber, Mable Akey, Eleanor Lambert, Dorothy Castine, Marcella Trombley, Helena G. Edwards, Dorothy Jessey, Caroline Prokop and Lillian McNulty.

Professional service extended into other arenas, as well. Women within the county have served in a number of capacities, ranging from medicine to the law, beauty shops to retail stores. Two of the most common positions held by women were those of telephone operator and postmaster. Included among those who worked for the United States Post Office throughout the county were Leslie Ryan, Ethel Ashline, Ruth Gagnier, Elsie Hazen, Deborah McGregor Shutt, Eva LeClair, Eliza Carpenter, Hazel Hoff, Gale Tourville, Oreina Lavoie, Rita Humphrey and Rosemary Kaufman. Offering another means of communication, operators helped to connect people via the telephone until the dial system took over. In Saranac, Hettie

Grant served as the operator. "In the front window of her home was the switchboard where she plugged in the calls as town folks cranked their wall phones, calling, 'Hello, Central?' or 'Hello, Hettie, get me so-and-so.'" Other telephone operators were Lucy Goodrow in Rouses Point and Champlain, Sadie Humphrey in Clinton, Blanche Crabtree in Ellenburg Depot, Blanch Watson Smith in Ellenburg Center and Blanch Crabtree Hogan, Mable Atkinson, Gladys Atkinson and Irene Bovia Longtin in Ellenburg after New York Telephone took over the telephone system. Many other women worked within the telephone industry and joined the telephone pioneers. They include Hazel Wells Webb, Alice Baker, Mary Mae Filion, Eulalia Dustin, Helen M. Siddon, Patricia Frances, Marjorie Crowder, Susan Childress and Genevieve Laundrie.

Among the various women who have owned retail shops within the county are Ruth Gagnier Whalen, Verda Lashway and Patsy Soper, all of whom owned beauty shops; Annette Decosse, Emma Blow and Rose Arno, all of whom ran general stores; and Margaret Finnecy, Ellen Finnecy, Delinne Perry, Mrs. Theodore Moise, Mary Patnode, Susan Cook, Maria Coe Flagg and Clarissa Winans Allen, all of whom worked as dressmakers, tailors or seamstresses. Other seamstresses include Miss Flagg and Miss Rogers, who, in 1820, advertised that they would accept grain, butter and sugar in trade. Another seamstress, Ruby Magoon, was remembered very fondly by Myra Magoon White:

> *She was a very able seamstress and in this way earned her living. She had the honor of sewing the stars on Ellenburg's Service Flag during the World War…She was devoted to her church and was a member in the M.E. Sunday School. She was an Epworth League and W.C.T.U. member. She taught school for a short time…She had a quiet and loving way and was universally loved and respected both in our town and surrounding towns. Children were especially fond of her for her kindness.*

Another member of the WCTU, Frances Hall was, according to the *Historical Sketches of the Town of Plattsburgh*, "a self-styled physician and a pharmacist who turned out patent medicine." Fanoline, her most famous patent medicine, was an ointment that Allen Everest "described as a healing antiseptic and curative ointment which was good for fever sores, piles, sore nipples, burns, chapped hands and lips, and much more." The ointment was patented circa 1890 and then marketed commercially, though it did not make a lot of money.

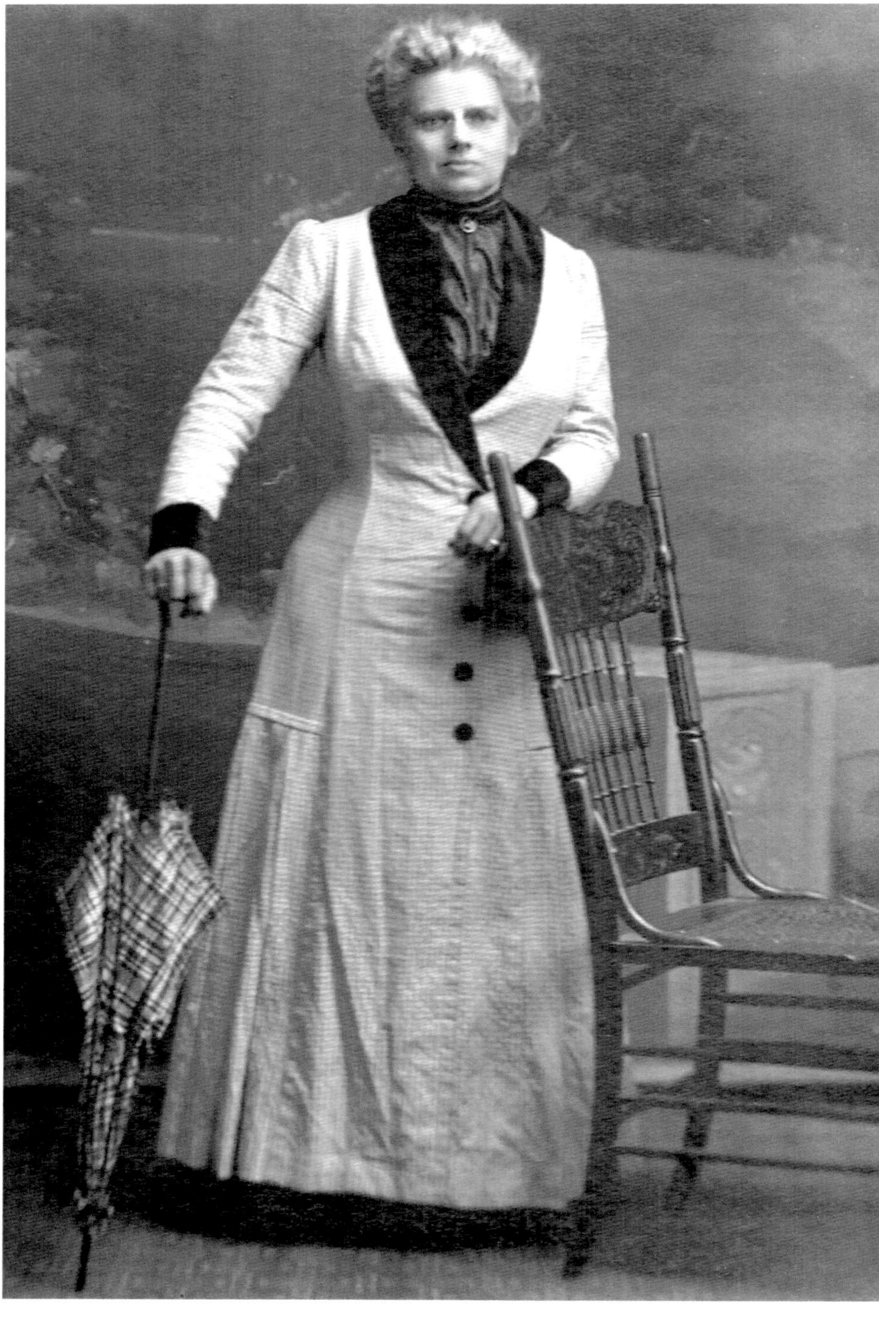

Frances Sanborn, a local teacher, businesswoman and caregiver. *Clinton County Historian's Office.*

Other women who have worked in customer service are Viola McDonald, Helen Wood, Marge Deso, Betty Sullivan, Grace Darrah, Hilda Lafontaine, Cassie Gerolimatos, Jane LaMare, Madeline Chasolen, Dawn Chicelli, Leona Gioiosa, Isabel LaBounty, Irene Row, Veronica Brushnefski, Marion Downs, Lillian de Celle, Juanita Beaucare, Ola Ashline, Viola Abraham, Marie Donah, Orissia Ducharme Hurt, Helen Bleeker, Pollyann Johnson, Shelley Bertrand, Elizabeth Caplan Kleppner, Doris Zielinski, Laura Beshaw, Regina Welch, Jean Anne Duchaine, Diane Fleming, Lois Brown, Gladys Trudeau and Judi DePaul. Some other women in the county went out on their own, selling for organizations like Avon, Mary Kay and Tupperware, including Barbara Cumm, Lillian Pelkey, Dorothy Berdan, Hazel Baker and Cassie McGee.

Women have worked in various aspects of the business world, and the Champlain Valley Business and Professional Women's Club seeks to educate, advocate for and support their work. Among the women who have been involved with business in the area are Elizabeth Kelly, Adore Flynn Kurtz, Sharlene Petro Durgan, Nancy Church, Carina Parrow, Joy Good, Vicki Marking, Weena Boyle, Stacey Hillman and Kelley Plummer.

Frances Sanborn offers an interesting final look at women and work. She worked in a mix of retail and human services settings. Frances is listed as receiving a twenty-five-dollar salary from the board of supervisors in 1895, presumably for teaching students; the next year, a society item on June 26, 1896, remarked, "Miss Frances Sanborn is conducting a kindergarten school at her home, where the troop of little ones gather with gleeful interest." During the same period, she wrote a history of Miss Frances E. Willard's life and actively participated in the Women's Christian Temperance Union that Willard founded. In 1907, she opened a ladies' furnishing store in Plattsburgh's Emery Block with Mrs. John Jersey. From that shop she regularly advertised the millinery work available, especially through society items in the *Plattsburgh Daily Press*, and traveled to New York City for inspiration and buying trips. However, Sanborn seems to have switched focus later in life. Throughout the 1930s, she is listed as caring for various women suffering from illnesses, in their homes or in her own.

Chapter 3

SCHOOL DAYS

An Overview of the System

Schools in Clinton County have taken on many forms, ranging from private schools held within homes to large, public institutions. What unites them, more than anything else, is their dedication to turning out qualified and informed individuals capable of contributing to the community. John W. Harrold, a longtime Clinton County educator and administrator, wrote a history of education in the county in 1980. His account points out that early settlers often banded together to provide education for children within the home: "Sometimes the children of two of more families would be grouped together by parents and taught in a home by a teacher engaged by the parents. Sometimes a teacher would hold a school in his or her own home, or some other building, and parents would pay for the service…In some communities where mill companies were located, a school was established and paid for by the mill company." New York State first provided for the support of schools in 1785, when schools were considered to be a function of the town and of the state, allowing the towns to levy taxes to support local schools and requiring the state to contribute to the cost of running the school. That amount was often not equal to the task of maintaining operations, though, so parents were regularly asked to pay an additional fee in order to send their children to the local school.

After New York State enacted a law in 1812 to provide for the creation of school districts across the state, these systems changed. Towns elected "school commissioners who, acting as a board, were empowered and directed to divide their respective towns into a suitable and convenient number of districts or establishing and keeping a school within each district. Whenever necessary, a district could be formed from areas in two adjoining towns when the school commissioners from the two towns mutually agreed to the formation of such a joint school district." This law paved the way for the eventual creation of more than two hundred small, one- and two-room schools throughout the county.

Yet the system was not ideal, so New York State refined its plan, creating the Union Free School Law of 1853. That law "permitted a single common school district, or a combination of two or more common school districts, on the affirmative vote of the inhabitants, to organize a union free school district." In the earlier system, voters at a district meeting could help to make decisions about the school and its operation; under the new law, district voters elected board members who would then undertake the governance of the school, including the establishment of rules for discipline, textbooks, grades and courses of study. Under this law, union free school districts could establish both secondary school programs (to train students for college entrance exams) and high schools. An 1867 act of the New York State legislature formed the Plattsburgh Union Free School District. Others followed in AuSable Forks, Cadyville, Chazy, Dannemora, Ellenburg Depot, Lyon Mountain, Mooers, Morrisonville, Peru, Rouses Point and West Chazy, with high schools present in all but West Chazy. Additionally, high schools were organized at Altona, Beekmantown and Saranac, though these were not part of union free districts.

The consolidation of these school districts began in 1904, supported by the Unification Act and the creation of the New York State Department of Education. In Clinton County, Chazy Central Rural School (CCRS) was the first example of a consolidated school district. Established in 1916, CCRS encompassed ten common school districts and the union free school district. Clara Soden, district superintendent of schools of the Third Supervisory District of Clinton County, oversaw the consolidation, which necessitated the construction of a new school building. That building, furnished by William H. and Alice T. Miner, was a state-of-the-art facility that included among its forty-four rooms two gymnasiums and swimming pools, modern toilet facilities and shower baths, science laboratories, industrial workshops, agricultural facilities, domestic science rooms, art studios, music rooms and a large auditorium, complete with a pipe organ and fully-equipped stage. Further changes in districts continued to occur until 1970.

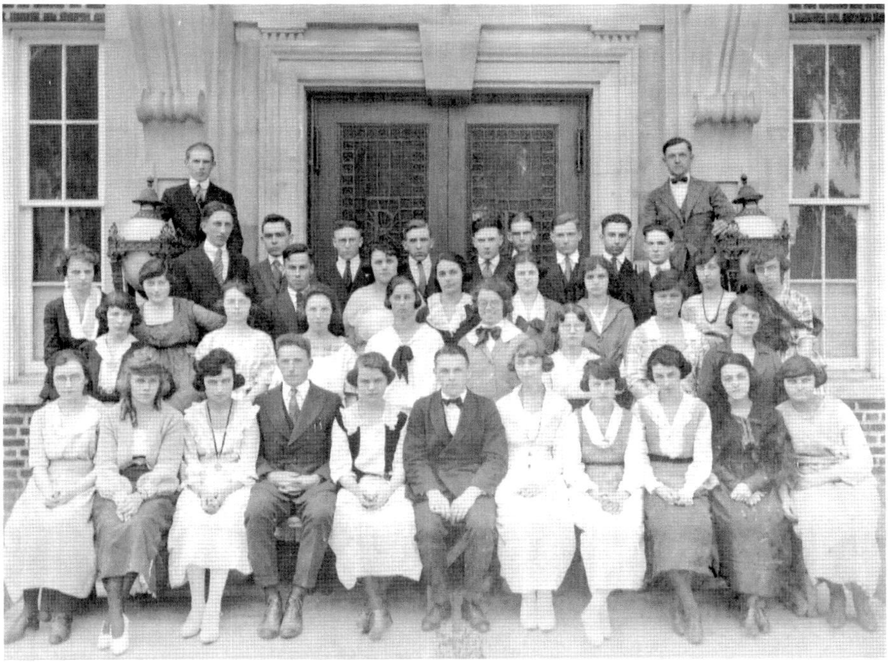

Plattsburgh High School Class of 1920. *Clinton County Historian's Office.*

One offshoot of this consolidation was the creation of the Board of Cooperative Educational Services (BOCES), which allowed students from across the county to complete vocational training as part of their high school curriculum. The facility that houses this program, though now known as CV-Tec, was originally named in honor of Harrold. Students are now able to complete training in several areas that include auto collision repair, automotive technology, aviation technology, construction trades, cosmetology, culinary arts management, digital art and design, early childhood education, medical office assisting, broadcasting technology, New Visions (for careers in law and government, healthcare or engineering) and welding.

Among the students who have benefitted from this specialized training are Samantha Crouse, Kellie Carter Duquette, Tonya Lashway Turner, Angel Facteau Drollette, Teena Rose, Elizabeth Dubray Baker, Lori Mancini Peryea, Laurie Castine Guay, Kim Dumas Simpson, Tracy Allen Gordon, Kelly Burke Katz, Dana Spooner, Vanessa Correll, Denise Martineau, Penny Merrill and Diane Besaw.

SCHOOL SYSTEMS

From the beginning of the nineteenth century, schools have existed in the county. Helena Augustine established the first kindergarten in the village of Plattsburgh in 1800, while Hannah Leonard started teaching classes in Rouses Point the following year. In Peru, the Union Academy followed in 1812. A two-story, frame building that stood on the Rogers Road, the academy was led by Chauncey Stoddard and his assistant Mary Rogers, with Lydia Rogers joining them as an instructor. Tuition at the academy, according to J. Warren Harkness, was $2.00 per quarter, though the addition of grammar as an area of study increased that cost to $2.50 per quarter. Boarding, with "respectable families," was also available to students at a cost of $1.20 a week.

Some progressive families were particularly dedicated to offering educational opportunities to their daughters. Allen Everest reminds us that Pliny Moore, for example, "saw to it that his children obtained the education that each wanted, consistent with his pocketbook and the six of the offspring. Thus, all of the later children attended elementary school in Champlain; then the girls attended boarding school elsewhere and came home, while the boys went to boarding school out of town and two of them obtained college degrees." His daughters carried on the tradition, with Anna going so far as to establish a private school for her daughter, niece and girls from the area in 1828 and 1829. She hired a teacher, paying two dollars a week plus keep, and established her home in Chazy as the school. Her sister Sophia continued the process, operating a school in her home in Champlain. Sophia's school attracted Frances Delord and the Davidson sisters away from the academy.

The Plattsburgh Academy emerged as an idea in 1811, when a committee that included several prominent men from the village of Plattsburgh accepted the task of raising money to purchase a suitable lot and build a schoolhouse, and was incorporated under this name in 1828. The building, though completed in 1811, was leased to the U.S. government and used as a barracks in the winters of 1813 and 1814 and then repurposed the following year. Miss Cook, who assisted the Reverend Frederick Halsey, and Miss Deming, who taught the ladies department until the fall of 1824, were part of the early faculty of the academy, which, according to Peter Sailly Palmer and the *Historical Sketches of Plattsburgh*, expanded in 1817 to include a school "for the instruction of young ladies in the various useful and ornamental branches of education" taught by Miss Clark. However, it was not until 1821 that the academy advertised the ladies' school, "under the superintendence of Miss Colt, in which young Ladies may, with superior advantages, be taught all the branches of science & literature, pertaining to a female education." One student of this institution, Frances Delord, was described as "a devout, loving, intelligent but submissive young lady whom all who knew her adored." In addition to Miss Deming's classes, which cost $2.50 a quarter by 1820, Delord also studied dance with Mrs. Deshons for $3.50. Another student of note, Margaret Davidson, became a gifted poet.

Over time, other schools joined the Plattsburgh Academy, offering both single-sex and coeducational options for girls. The Grey Nuns of the Cross, who came to Plattsburgh from Ottawa, opened their school, D'Youville Academy, on December 7, 1856, thus establishing the first parochial school in the region. Later, in 1863, the Saranac Academy opened, charging, by the term, $3.00 for "Common English," $4.00 for "Higher English," $2.50 for French and $10.00 for music with the use of an instrument. Among the academy's faculty members were Kate Stetson, a Champlain native and graduate of the Oswego Normal School, whose "presence is thought to be an acquisition to society and a benefit to the children under her care," and Miss Marshall, of whom a newspaper item explained, "We know our academy fathers could not fail to see the propriety of securing Miss Marshall's service. If good, live teachers are employed there will be no deficiency on the part of the pupils." Helena Augustin's Plattsburgh Kindergarten School, which opened in 1878 with fifteen students, marked the first concentrated effort to educate the youngest of area children.

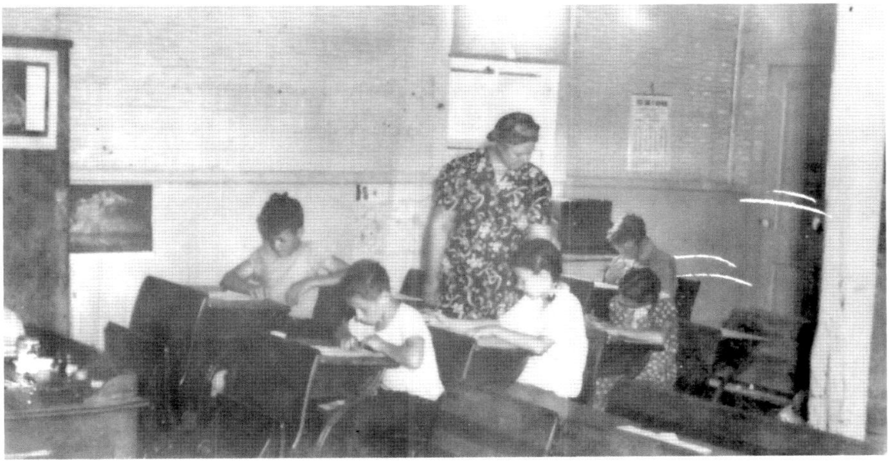

Teacher and students at Plattsburgh's School District No. 3, School No. 1, July 1949. *Clinton County Historian's Office.*

Along with larger academies, Clinton County included a large number of smaller schools, organized into districts and generally housed within one- or two-room schoolhouses that dotted the countryside and occupied a significant place in the lives and history of women. As Douglas Skopp explained in his history of Plattsburgh's Normal School, "The great majority of the nation's teaching corps—especially in the elementary and junior high schools, as well as the rural ungraded schools—were women. A perfectly qualified woman teacher who married, however, instantly was excluded from any teaching position. Her loyalty and duty, it was believed, should and would go to her husband and her own family." He continued, writing, "Because unmarried women were dependent upon finding a teaching position for their own livelihood, they often had to accept low-paying contracts out of necessity. Moreover, there was no tenure after a probationary period; contracts were renewed from year to year, based on the number of children in the school. Often, a teacher had to have some special connection or relationship to the superintendent or local school board to secure a contract in the first place, and draw on these connections every year for its renewal."

Among the women who served as teachers throughout the county were Mary Emmonds, the first teacher in the town of Clinton; Catherine Mason, who retired in 1880 after serving as the Oak Street School teacher for almost thirty years; Emily Arnold, who taught in the "old red school house on the Keeseville Plains"; Minnie Murphy, in Hallock Hill; and Josie and Jennie Casey, both of whom taught at Pickett's Corners. Alice Lamkins, who taught in Clayburg, was lauded for the high enrollment in the school, with the local press writing, on February 27, 1882, "School under Miss Alice Lamkins is filled to overflowing, which is creditable to the teacher, as the Academy school usually reduces our attendance in this district." Susie Hunter taught in the Peasleeville, Durginville, Patent, Norrisville, Henry Devins and Dean Charles schools—all in and around Peru; she sometimes rode horseback to her post and other times stayed with a family near the school.

Mary Tagan Gadway, known as Mollyee, offers an interesting look at the transition from rural to central schools. In 1928, Gadway interviewed with a trustee of School District #20 in Merrill. She rejected his first offer of twenty dollars a week for teaching, so he increased his offer to twenty-three dollars, and she accepted the position. Mollyee wrote, for *Ellenburg Yesterday and Today*, "I had never been in a rural school before I taught in one. I had all grades from 1st to 8th. It was a very large group of children—several beginners and several getting ready to take Regents exams. The children took their regents at Lyon Mountain High School. I enjoyed the Rural School very much.

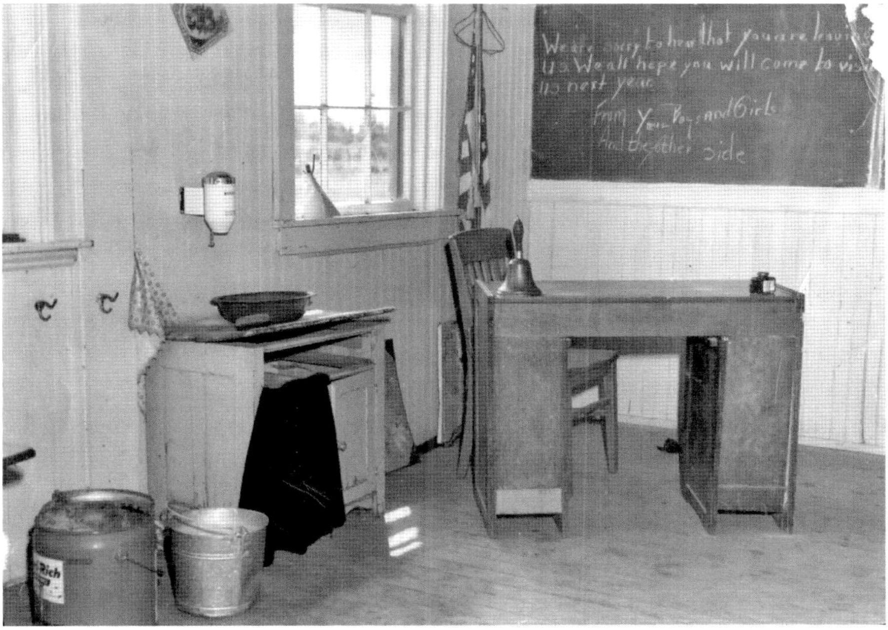

A word of thanks for the departing teacher. *Clinton County Historian's Office.*

I taught in District #20 for 25 years. We called it Lake View because we had such a beautiful view of Chateaugay Lake." After that, she was able to teach kindergarten at Northern Adirondack Central School, in Ellenburg Corners, returning to the position for which she had trained as a student. Even after retiring in 1974, Gadway continued as an educator, serving as a substitute teacher for the elementary school at NACS until 1984.

Teachers are remembered for many reasons. Some, like Rachael Burt, are recalled for their quirky personalities or actions. According to Sarah Baker, Burt "used a crutch which she often flung the length of the schoolroom aimed at some disorderly boy. Her aim rarely missed." Dora Warren was remembered as a good teacher, though sarcastic; she "laid great stress on proper English and taught grammar with the aid of a ruler." Grace Vandervoost was known as "a kind but serious teacher. Never known to smile." Conversely, Gertrude and Grace Barker, teachers at Plattsburgh High School, are remembered as being "completely awesome." And teachers like Mary Lou Zaferakis, an eighth grade math teacher and principal at Peru Central School, evoke memories of good humor and grace. Among the many activities for which she is recalled are her active participation in

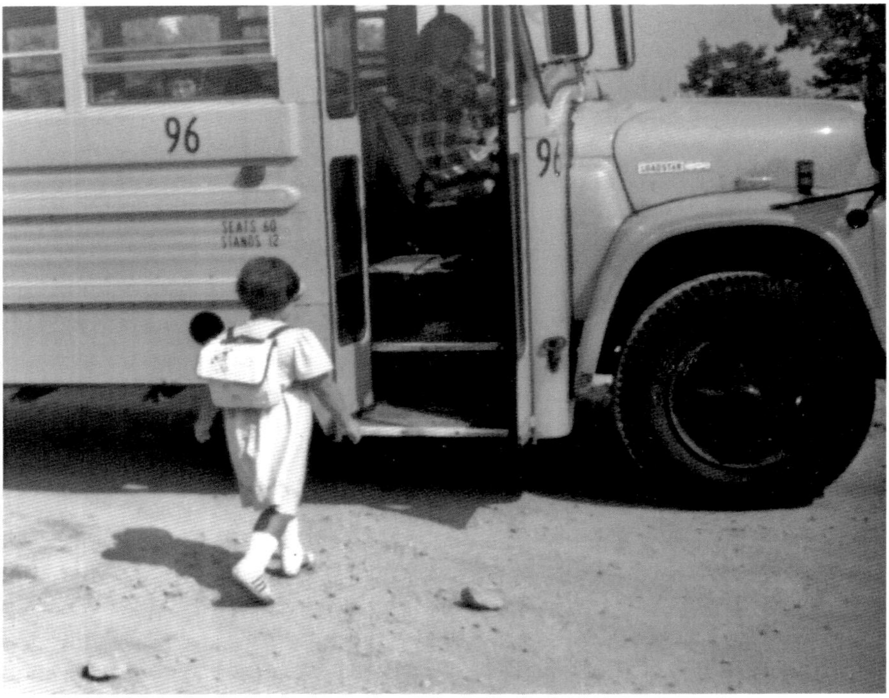

The author boards the bus driven by Miss Linda on her first day of school, 1980. *Author's collection.*

extracurricular events, her ability to make lessons accessible and interesting and her commitment to her family and church.

Those teachers were not alone in their service to local students. A veritable army of people is required to run and maintain a school and a school district. Among the other women who have supported local education through their work as teacher's aides, school nurse teachers, school librarians, school bus drivers, secretaries, maintenance personnel, board of education members, lunchroom monitors, cafeteria staff and parent-teacher organization members and in extracurricular programs are: Crystal Simpson, a bus driver who regularly purchased winter jackets, hats and mittens for students on her run; Carol Patnode; Beatrice Curran; Carol Allen, who supervised the Peru Jr.-Sr. High School cafeteria, providing nourishing meals for students; Sophia Jones; Lynn Corde; Jane and Bonnie Harblin, who served as lunchroom monitors in Peru, often making students feel special through their lunchtime conversations; Agnes LaFontaine Frennier; Sophia Jones; Yvette Gough; Dawn Irwin; Pamela Torrance Sears; Tina Simpson; Mae Poissant; June

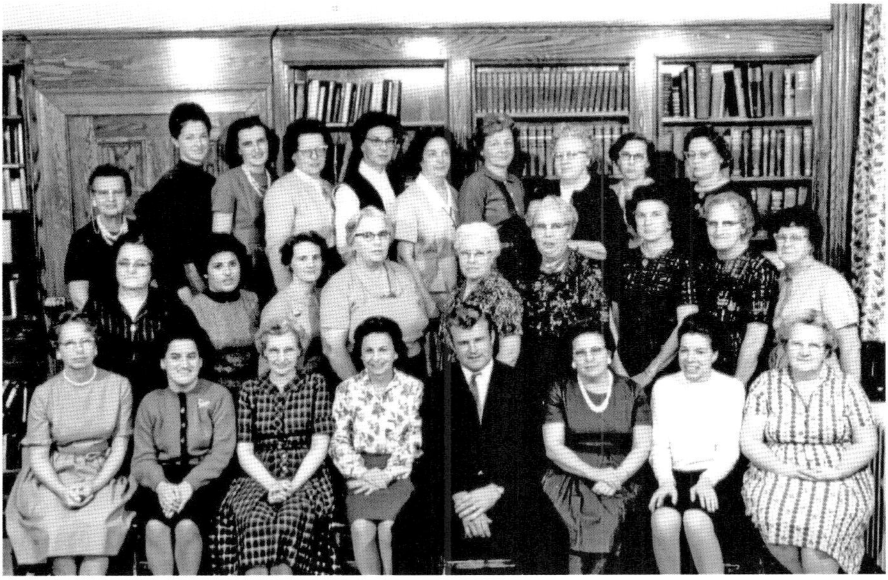

Teachers, including Leah Drown, at the Ellenburg Central School District. *Leah Drown.*

Heming; Phyllis Clausen; Patti Bentley; Rosemary Souza-Botten; Cathy LaFontaine; Sally Ryan; Mary Stein; Mary Patnode; Catherine Normandin; Annette Hosler; Megan Briddell; Kim Ladue; Jennifer Parliament; Nancy Vesco; Ann Capen; Kathy Wilson; Amy Belair; Charlene Favaro; Michelle Duprey Timmons; Caren Murray Laundrie; Laura Marlow; Donna Kemp; Gail Kemp; Kathy Dupraw; Kim Barnes; Jody Dumas; Cheryl Deso; Mary LaPierre; Marianne Garrow; Kate Dermody; Elizabeth "Biz" Green; Julie Coon; Melissa Niquette; Alison Grovine; Joan Seidel; Cheryl Phillips; Karen Reynolds; Jaye Riddle; Maria Rafalko; Christine Devins; Grace Trombley; Lauren Whitehouse; Anna Cesar; and Elaine Leavitt.

HIGHER EDUCATION

Many of the women who taught within Clinton County attended the Plattsburgh Normal School (PNS), which later became part of the state university and which was the subject of Douglas Skopp's book, *Bright with Promise*. The normal school was founded in 1889, after New York State passed a Normal School Act (1866) and Plattsburgh's senator, Stephen

Moffitt, introduced a bill (Chapter 517, New York State Laws of 1889) "to establish a Normal and Training School at the village of Plattsburgh," where students at the normal school could practice their newly acquired teaching skills on the young students of the Training School, working under the supervision of instructors. At the start, tuition, books and railroad fare were free for New York State residents who completed the twenty-week term, with the school requesting only that students bring any books that might supplement the library's meager collection. In return, they earned a diploma that allowed them "to teach in any of the public schools in this state for life." By 1911, students had to declare which of two courses of study they would pursue: the "Professional Course," which, as "the forerunner of the present liberal arts programs at the College…prepared the student for a career in an elementary or secondary public school, with an emphasis upon a specific teaching skill, area or discipline," or the "Commercial Course," "which prepared the student to teach business related subjects in a high school." The Normal School officially became the Plattsburgh State Teachers' College (PSTC) in 1942 and moved to a curriculum in which four-year programs led to bachelor's degrees. PSTC joined the SUNY system in 1948 and eventually came to be known as SUNY Plattsburgh or Plattsburgh State University (PSU), one of the thirteen comprehensive colleges and the sixty-four academic institutions included within SUNY.

Although women were among the instructors from the beginning of the institution, they received salaries that were considerably lower than those of their male counterparts. While George H. Hudson, who would later become principal of PNS, earned $1,500 for teaching natural science, Thankful M. Knight (the only member of the Department of Methods) received $900; Sara J. Stewart (principal of the training school) received $800; Mary W. Lyon (the entire Department of English Literature and History), Alice O'Brien (the only member of the Department of Elocution and Physical Culture) and both Eliza Kellas and Elizabeth Garrity (teachers in the training school) each received $700; and Helen M. Palmer (the entire Department of French and German) received $500. Yet, when his much-loved niece, Theodora Kyle, was hired in 1892 to teach history and rhetoric at PNS, David Kellogg believed that "she has done splendidly. There is hardly a girl in her college class that has so good a place. One girl has $800 per year in Providence, but hardly another one had $700."

Among the many teachers at PNS, Eliza Kellas was noted by the American Association of University Women "for her exacting scholarship and logical thinking. She was tireless in her ambition and always innovative. She liberalized the school and she stressed science education for women. She actively recruited students from outside the immediate geographical area. She developed a house-mother system for the dormitories, and she put up student government, and emphasized student responsibility. She began a program of extensive renovation and expansion of the campus." Born on a farm near Mooers Forks, Kellas attended the Potsdam Normal School, graduating in 1889. She became the principal of the Intermediate Department and Methods teacher at PNS in 1891, eventually becoming preceptress, or dean of students. Eliza returned to school, studying at Radcliffe College in 1911, nine years after resigning from PNS, and then served as headmistress of the Emma Willard School in Troy and the first dean of Russell Sage College.

Many of PSU's faculty members have been recognized for their service to the college, to the community and to their students. Dr. Daphne Kutzer, for example, was promoted to the rank of SUNY Distinguished Teaching Professor in 2003; a member of the English faculty, she focuses on children's literature, writing by women, nineteenth-century literature and critical theory. Dr. Mary Roden-Tice, a geologist, was appointed to the same rank in 2013. Roden-Tice was described as "a dedicated and tireless teacher, prodigious and creative scholar and caring member of the college community at SUNY Plattsburgh for 19 years" in Chancellor Nancy Zimpher's recommendation to the board of trustees. Gerianne Wright explained that Roden-Tice, an earlier recipient of the Chancellor's Award for Excellence in Teaching (2001), "is a world-class scholar who involves her students in every aspect of her work, first by instilling a sense of curiosity and wonder, and then by carefully mentoring them through the intricacies of the research." Diane Fine was named SUNY Distinguished Teaching Professor in 2011, earning the honor for her work as a printmaker and teacher on the art faculty, while Dr. Nancy J. Church, of the entrepreneurship faculty, received the professorship in 2004 and the Chancellor's Award for Excellence in Teaching in 1992. While they are not the only respected, loved and distinguished faculty members at Plattsburgh State, these women offer a glimpse of the faculty's excellence and of the role women continue to play on campus, where issues of pay inequity faded with the development of standardized salaries across SUNY.

Students at PNS and, later, PSU, are also noted for their contributions to their chosen professions and to their communities. One such student, Helen Carpenter Blow, was born in Ellenburg Center, graduated from the Normal School in 1933 and then taught in rural schools for nine years before teaching at Ellenburg Central School for another two years. Another, Beatrice Morrison, graduated from PNS in 1938, later earning a bachelor's degree and then a Master of Library Science at Syracuse University. Putting her training to use, Morrison served as the K-12 school librarian at Altona Central School before becoming the elementary school librarian when the Northern Adirondack Central School was formed. Beatrice did not stop with those jobs, though; instead, she supervised the dramatic club, spent four summers as the Bookmobile Librarian for the Clinton-Essex Library Service, helped to catalogue and set up Saranac's high school library and spent four summers as the Campus School librarian at PSU. Julia Harrigan, a 1907 graduate, earned notoriety for a different reason: her commencement speech, titled "Municipal Ownership and Public Ownership," advocated socialism for the common good.

While a student at PSU, Susan Ouellette, who went on to earn advanced degrees from the University of Massachusetts, wrote a paper about Clara Lydia Dunster, another PNS student. In that paper, which is reprinted in *Bright with Promise*, she relays Dunster's feelings on the entrance exam (it "was quite hard. I don't know whether I passed or not, hope I did."), on the place ("I wish you could see all the nice stores, houses and churches here…I wish you could hear the folks talk French here, almost everyone does, even the little children…"), on women's rights (praising a friend "who has done what the organization of women's rights are always threatening. She has married and asked her husband to take her name, instead of losing her own identity in his.") and on teaching ("my objective is not at all to give [the pupil] knowledge, but to teach him how to acquire it as he may need it, to make him estimate it at its exact worth and to make him learn.") Ouellette's retelling of this history underscores the importance of women as makers and tellers of history.

In fact, several historians from Clinton County graduated from either PNS or PSU. Most famous among them is Marjorie Lansing Porter (1912), the first Clinton County historian and later the historian for the city of Plattsburgh and for Essex County. Addie Lawrence Shields (town of Beekmantown historian) and Iris Barcomb (town of Ellenburg historian) also graduated from the Normal School, while Margaret Nolan (town of Black Brook historian) earned a bachelor's degree in general studies from PSU in 1989, after working steadily, one or two courses a semester, from 1968 on.

Other graduates of these schools include Gladys Stratton, Alice Gildersleeve, Hazel Wells Webb, M. Margaret Ryan, M. Genevieve Douglass, Barbara Hale, Eileen McGaulley, Frances Boas, Dorothy Butler, Eveline Brothers, Marion Osier, Camellia Provost, Julia Miller, Edith Moss, Iva Goodspeed, Alice Webb, Helen Weir, C. Frances Hobbs, Hazel Baker, Lois Therrien and Pearl Brown.

SPECIALIZED TRAINING

Of course, PSU is not the only option for women who want to continue their education. Clinton Community College (CCC), established in 1966 and accredited in 1975, offers an excellent education for students wishing to complete an associate's degree. Though CCC offers a number of degree options, its nursing program is one of the most popular among women. As one of the occupations traditionally open to women, nursing offered a means to a career, a vocation or a job between school and marriage. Clinton's two-year nursing program, which leads to an applied associates of science degree, prepares students to sit for the State Board of Licensing Examination in Registered Professional Nursing and, with successful completion of that exam, to receive the registered nurse (RN) license.

Both the Physicians Hospital and the Champlain Valley Hospital (CVH) also offered nursing programs in the area. The CVH School of Nursing opened in 1910, with students both studying and living in the building next to the hospital. Students completed three years of study before earning their registered nursing credential. Run by the Grey Nuns, the Champlain Valley Hospital School of Nursing operated from 1910, with an official charter by the New York State Board of Regents in 1913, until 1972 and served about 1,200 students. A similar hospital-based school of nursing was operated

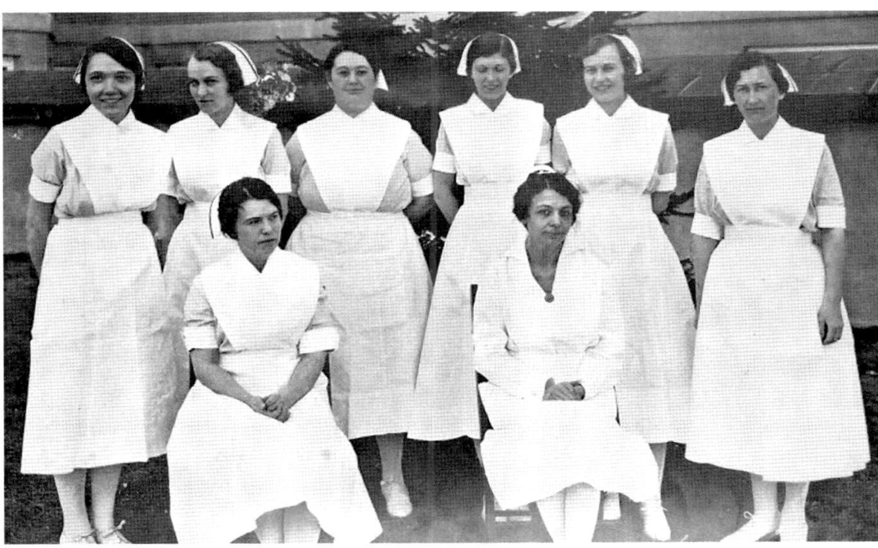

Nursing faculty at the Physicians Hospital School of Nursing, 1931. *Clinton County Historian's Office.*

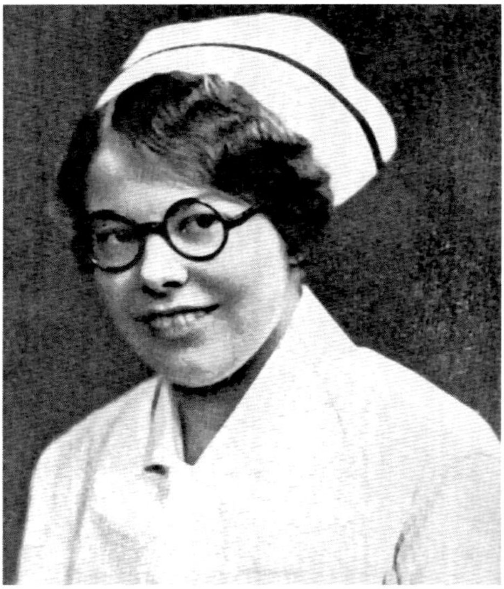

Gladys Gray Bradley, of West Plattsburgh, graduated from the Physicians Hospital in 1931. *Clinton County Historian's Office.*

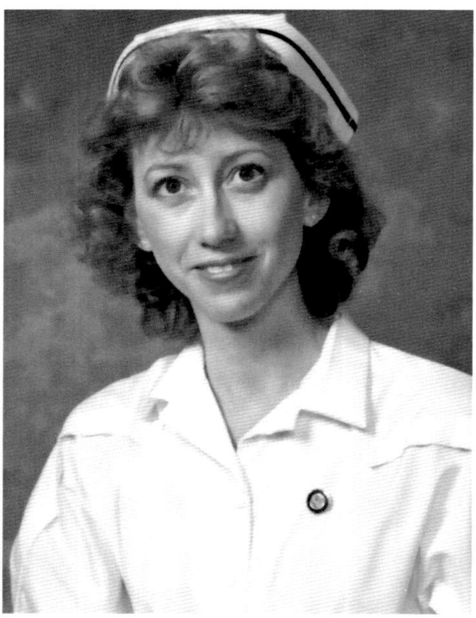

Nita Deyo, who, after serving in the Air Force, graduated from Clinton Community College's Nursing Program in the early 1990s. *Author's collection.*

at the Physicians Hospital from 1913 until the two hospitals merged in 1972. The resultant merger produced the Champlain Valley Physicians Hospital and its School of Nursing, which closed in June 1979.

Graduates of the local hospital nursing and college-based programs include D. Shirley Light, Gloria Long, Joyce Hamilton, Bernadette Brown, Marceline Kavanagh, Lisa Wells, Alice Repas, Sister Mary Loretta Bechard, Mary McClellan, Pauline Mischler, Naomi Pettis Bell, Lore Lamora Robinson, Cristin Cleary Mills, Alice Hamell Repas, Ruth Rohrbach, Patricia Welch, Nancy Gioiosa, Alice Coste Schurr, Hazel Kahn, Heide Purtell, Christine LaMar and Mary Kavanagh.

Other specialized training is available through Champlain Valley Educational Services, which offers—among other possibilities—courses for adults to enter the field of healthcare as licensed practical nurses (LPNs), certified nurse's aides (CNAs), EKG technicians and phlebotomy technicians. The CVPH School of Radiologic Technology, established in 1965 under the guidance of Fay Ashline, offers a different path to healthcare, training students to work as X-ray technicians in a two-year program that allows the students to sit for the American Registry of Radiologic

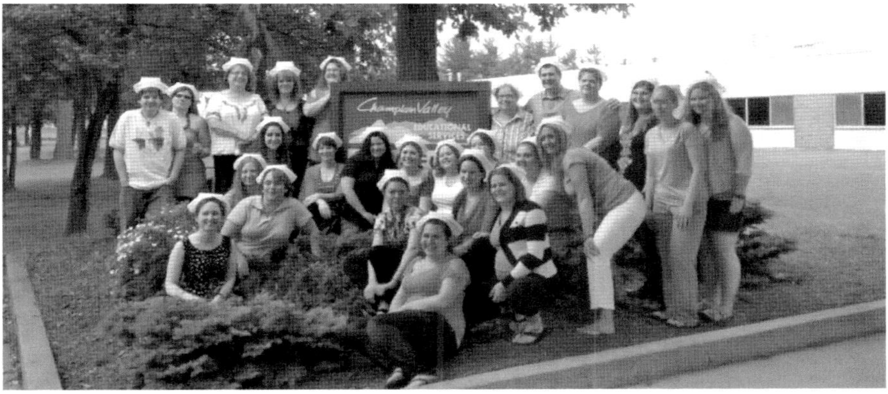

Licensed Practical Nurses from CV-Tec's 2013 graduating class. *Christa Covel Reyell.*

Technologists Registry Exam and, upon successful completion of that exam, to be licensed radiologic technologists.

Some local women who work in various aspects of health and human services, having completed these or other educational programs, include Marla Garcia, Sheila Bull, Christa Covel Reyell, Stacie Altman Beck, Sara Seymour St. Louis, Kelly Regan Ahern, Cristi Polhemus Wells, Valdoraise Conway, Florence Pelkey, Clara Pollock, Dora Phaneuf Sears, Stella Hickey, Lila Covey Moulton, Adelaide Pray, Marjorie Coolidge St. Louis, Aldora McDonald, Donna Montgomery, Rita Humphrey, Lorraine Smith, Helen Coulter, Rita Abare, Cosette Aspinall, Eileen McCaffrey, Susan Blair Conover, Katherine Haley, Catherine O'Connell, Deanna Wilson, Anne Islas Heywood, Lynn Barcomb James, Michelle Posada Daniels, Anja Rothhaar Bouchard, Eileen Roach, Ellie Douglass, Elizabeth Brewster, Nicole Reome Devins, Karen Stiles Titherington, Lori Slattery Keever, Carrie Scott LaFountain, Sarah Akey Mitchell, Doris Higgins Covert, Holly Kipp, Rachel Patrie Miller, Mabel Stratton, Susan Latinville, Cora Apperson, Ellie Murray, Patricia Aldous, Marjorie Boswell, Catherine Sells, Diane Davis, Alice Sherman, Rachel Stone and Nicole Pratt Coskey.

Another Clinton County native who made an impact on the world of healthcare through her advanced education was Lucy Hobbs Taylor. Born in Ellenburg in 1833, Taylor went west at the age of sixteen and worked in Michigan as a seamstress and teacher. Because most medical schools had adopted a "no women" policy, she arranged an internship with a dentist—not an easy task—and became competent enough to practice dentistry, which did not require a diploma at the time. Taylor entered the Ohio College of Dentistry in 1865, after having worked in offices in Cincinnati and Iowa, and graduated on February 21, 1865, the first woman to graduate from an accredited dental college as a doctor of dental surgery. Lucy continued to practice in Chicago and then in Kansas, working until her death in 1910. The American Association of Women Dentists established an award in her honor in 1983, and in 1999, a New York State historic marker was erected in her honor.

Business and Industry

Women who preferred to go into the world of business and clerical work—as secretaries, stenographers, sales clerks and business owners—were able to choose among the Plattsburgh Business Institute (PBI) and the Loretta Business Institute (LBI), which later became Our Lady of Victory Secretarial School. These schools offered a practical means of learning a trade and, sometimes, of finding a vocation.

When it opened in 1930, the Plattsburgh Business Institute announced its offerings in the May 23 *Plattsburgh Sentinel*, explaining the school provided "a well equipped and up-to-date commercial school, affording thorough training, where young men and women might pursue a practical course of study, at a minimum cost, and at the same time to qualify themselves to fill the ever growing positions that are offered the commercial trained person of the day." Samuel Todd, with twenty-five years of teaching experience, including seventeen as the associate head of the Commercial Teachers Training Department at the Plattsburgh Normal School, was to lead the endeavor, which offered a full commercial course as well as a full secretarial course and preparation for civil service exams. By 1931, PBI was advertising additional courses, including shorthand and typing. Sadly, in 1957, PBI announced its closure, citing prohibitive costs as a reason to end operations. Over its twenty-eight-year history, PBI graduated some six hundred young men and women, most of whom were successful in their job searches because of their training.

The complete list of women who attended PBI is too long to reproduce here. However, some of the students who sought training in this school are Marie Brown, Grace Burleigh, Loretta Corron and Frances Todd, all of Plattsburgh High School's class of 1937; Pauline Lyons, of St. John's Academy's class of 1937; Mary Hart; Marguerite O'Connell; Dorothy McDonough; Shirley Duval; and Katharine Graham.

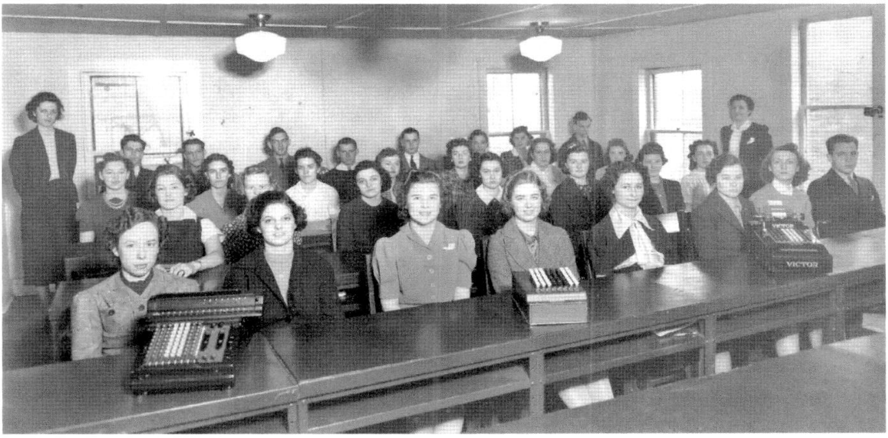

Teachers Genevieve Lyons and Margaret Sullivan with the 1939 graduating class of the Plattsburgh Business Institute. *Clinton County Historian's Office.*

When PBI closed, women interested in pursuing a commercial course were able to apply to the Loretta Business Institute (LBI), operated by the Religious Sisters of Mercy. Offering similar secretarial training, LBI was transferred to the Sisters of Charity of Saint Louis in 1958, becoming Our Lady of Victory Secretarial School, which continued to serve local students until 1993. Sister Theresa Martel, the executive director of OLV Secretarial School from 1965 until its closure, explained that some three thousand students attended the school during her tenure. Their curriculum changed as business technologies evolved, moving from manual typewriters, ditto machines and four-row keyboarding to computer keyboarding and word processing. One student who attended the school, Renée Strack, praised the institution for its work in a May 31, 1993 *Plattsburgh Press-Republican* article. She said, "Sister Martel helped me a lot as well as the other girls. She always pushed me to do my best in everything. She worked us hard and if was not perfect, she would make us do it again. She taught us not just how to type, but how to handle an intelligent conversation that will benefit us in our jobs."

Other women who attended either the Loretta Business Institute or the Our Lady of Victory Secretarial School include Catherine Mary, Beatrice Ryan and Betty Carter (St. John's Academy's class of 1937); Ester Grimshaw (Chazy Central Rural School's class of 1957); Amy Gudin Gonya; Carla Ducharme Matthews; Laurie St. Louis Baker; Nicole LaFountain O'Neill; Kimberly Parrotte Couture; Frances Schlichter; Marion Bouyea Miller; Veronica Runyan; and M. Frances Sumbler.

With the 1993 closure of the OLV Secretarial School, students interested in pursuing careers in business had to either leave the area in order to train or attend Clinton Community College, which offers a business track.

Chapter 4

SERVING A LOVED COMMUNITY

Service to the community has run through every facet of Clinton County life, from our earliest moments. A variety of volunteer organizations have helped to teach girls to contribute to their home, even while enjoying the region's many attractions. Chief among these groups is the Girl Scouts.

Girl Scouts

Developed by Juliette Gordon Low in 1912 and chartered by the United States Congress in 1950, Girls Scouts of the USA centers on a mission of building courage, confidence and character in girls who will "make the world a better place." Bevera Louden Bell, longtime executive director of the North Country Girl Scout Council, explained the significance of Girl Scouting:

> *Unless you are personally involved in Girl Scouting, most Americans think Girl Scouts is camping, cookies, badges, giggles and freckles. It's all this and much more. Times have changed and Girl Scouting has moved forward with today's changing girls by providing an innovative way to meet their needs. Girl Scouting provides the means to ensure tomorrow's young women will take the lead in our world. Girls learn to make responsible decisions, work in partnership with adults, study math, science and technology. They also participate in programs that promote self-esteem, deal with the pain of*

death and dying, the prevention of youth suicide, the skill of staying safe, the value of different cultures, the prevention of drug and alcohol abuse, the appreciation of Mother Earth, and the pride in being and doing her best. In addition, and of great importance, is the avenue provided for each girl to learn about herself, her community and her world.

Little did I know when I joined Brownies over 40 years ago, said the promise and accepted the law, where this opportunity would lead me. As a young girl, I remember overcoming shyness through my experiences in Girl Scouting. I recall feeling special because the Girl Scout advantage allowed me to meet new friends, attend fun-filled programs, and to relate with wonderful women in my home town of Champlain. I remember with great fondness some of my leaders, Mrs. Zurlo, Mrs. Pettinger, Mrs. Willette and Mrs. Walker, women I admired as a girl and hold in high regard today. I owe them, and others, a large thank you for playing an important role in my formative years, for giving of their time and talent to influence the lives of other women's daughters.

Girl Scout leaders certainly serve as beacons of community spiritedness and volunteerism. One woman who should be remembered is Dorothy

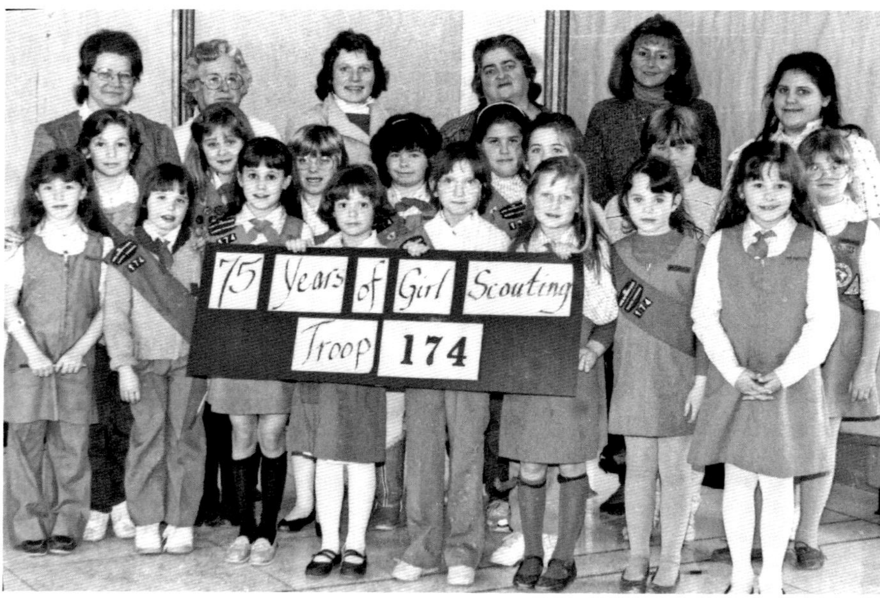

Peru Girl Scout troop, circa 1986, led by Judi DePaul, Mildred Desso, Nancy Jarvis, Gloria Pratt and Shelley Bertrand (left to right). *Author's collection.*

Marshall Johnson, who served as the leader of Plattsburgh's first Girl Scout troop. Johnson agreed to volunteer after being approached by the president of the Young Women's League in 1918. The troop included about twelve girls, aged ten to early teens, who worked to earn badges according to the printed requirements sent from the New York headquarters and later according to the official books published by the Girl Scouts organization.

Edna Jerry led the city's second troop, starting about 1920. When talking to the *Press-Republican*, Johnson, who spent more than twenty years volunteering with the Girl Scouts, explained that, "although the early troops performed many services to the community including rolling bandages," camping was the highest priority of early local Girl Scouts. The official camping costume in the early part of the twentieth century was "a pair of camp bloomers and a long blouse," and the camping experience included several trips to town every Sunday so that girls could attend their own churches. She endorsed the organization, saying, "I thought in the beginning, and I think now, that the Girl Scouts offers a wonderful opportunity for American girls...Of course, nowadays, troops, leaders and the organization as a whole, are all much better organized. But believe me, they couldn't have any more fun than we had in those early days of Scouting. And despite all the 'new' activities in Scouting, the latest generation couldn't possibly have as many fingers in the past as we had."

Another Girl Scout leader, Gloria Cusson Pratt, was honored by the North Country Girl Scout Council as the 1986 Leader of the Year. Nominated by three of her fellow Peru Girl Scout leaders, Susan Spissinger, Peggy Bureta and Claire Dalton, Gloria—my mother—was noted for her commitment to community service and her special connection to the girls in her troop. More than eighteen letters of support from the parents of girls, her parish priest, fellow leaders and Brownies accompanied her nomination. One of the Brownies, Darcy Filiatrault, asserted, "My leader Gloria Pratt should be leader of the year, because I love her. She is fun!" Another girl in the troop, Kathryne Murray, wrote, "I think Mrs. Pratt should be elected Girl Scout leader of the year because she is kind, friendly, and works hard to do her best. She also helps when I have a problem." The adults who supported the application noted similar traits. Darcy's mother, Debby Filiatrault, described Gloria as "a special lady," who loves children and is loved by children. "So many times," she wrote, "we don't have a choice as to who will be helping to mold our children's characters, their morals, etc. I'm very happy that Gloria is one of those teachers. My daughter is shy and unsure of herself at times. I have seen Gloria in action working with her, talking with her, boosting her

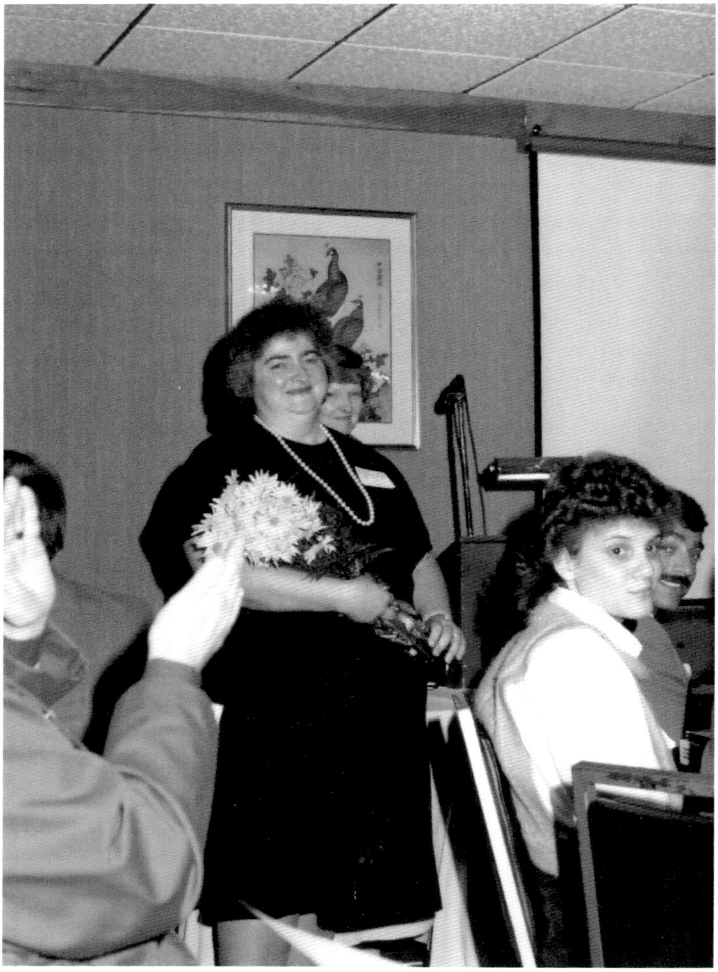

Gloria Pratt receiving the Girl Scout Leader of the Year award.
Author's collection.

confidence. It takes a lot of patience and love of which Gloria has a lot of both." Kathryne's mother, Diana Murray, wrote, "Gloria is genuinely concerned for the welfare of the girls in her troop. Each girl in Brownie Troop 174 is made to feel special and is encouraged to feel good about herself. Gloria is respected and well-liked by her Brownies."

The criteria for the Leader of the Year award, the highest council award, is outstanding service to girls. Gloria's nomination highlighted the many ways in which she provided such outstanding service. The application cites her focus on the individual child, encouragement of leadership skills and provision for individual contributions and growth. "Her patience, consideration, compassion, and love for children are evident in everything she does," the nomination continues. "Her confidence and encouragement in her girls' abilities creates an exciting learning environment. Enthusiasm for and love of children is clear—and contagious." Among the activities that Gloria undertook with her troop were Girl Scout Sunday at St. Augustine's Church in Peru, where she also taught religious education classes during the year and Bible Safari programs in the summer; fundraisers for the Peru Library Building Fund; the creation of the Brownie Kazoo Band that marched in local parades; and the "adoption" of Valehaven Nursing Home. Under Gloria Pratt's guidance, girls visited the nursing home regularly, bringing with them gifts for the residents (table favors, lapel flowers, etc., usually designed for an upcoming holiday), songs and a concern for the welfare of those living in the facility.

Since, as Peggy Bureta pointed out in her letter of recommendation, "scouting was unavailable to Gloria as a child…she vowed that the opportunity she missed would be there for her children. She loves Girl Scouting and all that it stands for, and intends to remain a Brownie leader for many years." In fact, my mom continued as a Brownie troop leader for several years after my sister and I moved up to the Girl Scouts and Cadets. Through example, she taught a generation of Peru Central School girls how to serve their community. As Susan Spissinger, another leader who inspired countless local girls, said, "As a model for other leaders she exemplifies the very best in girl Scouting—service, to God and country, helping people, being fair and honest, ever cheerful, friendly and considerate, using resources wisely, helping where needed, being a sister to her sister leaders, respecting others and protecting the world around her."

Other local Girl Scout leaders, den mothers for the Boy Scouts and 4-H leaders include N. Madeline Nichols, M. Genevieve Douglas, Valeda LaDuke, Florence Baade Sunderland, Margaret Colby Collins, Dorothy Ashline, Katherine Camp, Ethel Pray, Anne Erickson Allen, Bernice Lafontaine, Frances Baker, Elizabeth Mero, Shelley Bertrand, Mildred Desso, Nancy Jarvis, Sue Devins, Peggy Bureta, Claire Dalton, Sue Foole and Judi DePaul.

Since 1985, the local Girl Scout organization has also recognized Women of Distinction. Part of a national program to honor women for "their strength of character, dedicated community service, emphasis on life-long learning, [and]…dedication to fostering self-confidence and leadership skills in others." Four awards are given:

- Distinguished Trailblazer, which "honors a woman who has a proven track record of reaching ambitious or unconventional goals demonstrated by upward career mobility, steady growth and leadership skills. She is willing to take risks, inspires and motivates others. She has 'broken glass ceilings,' overcome and excelled under extreme challenges and demonstrated perseverance."
- Distinguished Community Leader, which honors "a woman who has demonstrated outstanding contributions over a period of time to her community. She is a role model, community leader, mentor, or has broken new ground. She is an agent for change who has made a measurable difference to those around her."
- Distinguished Personal Achievement, which "honors a woman who lives her life in such a way to serve others, both through her career and volunteer activities. She is a leader and an inspiration to others in all aspects of her life. She is willing to take risks and pursue activities that she believes in. It is by her example that others are motivated to take action."
- Distinguished Leader of Tomorrow, which honors a woman between the ages of seventeen and twenty-one "who is/was a Girl Scout and has demonstrated outstanding leadership ability and has contributed to her school and community. She has spearheaded a project or program to improve quality of life."

Among the local recipients of these awards have been Morgan McKinney (2008), a graduate of Plattsburgh High School who completed her senior year at Clinton Community College (CCC), achieving highest honors and earning spots on the President's List and the National Dean's List before going to Wellesley College, and Christine Darrah (2014), who graduated from AuSable Valley High School, earned an associate's degree at CCC and then entered the Champlain Valley Physicians Hospital School of Radiologic Technology. These two young women have made significant contributions to the region. McKinney established a scholarship at CCC and has completed significant community service at organizations as varied as the Lake Champlain Research Institute, the Elmore SPCA and the Special Olympics; Darrah created a donation center for Tropical Storm Irene, collecting money and goods to assist local residents affected by the storm. Others who have been honored are Theresa Bennett, Janet Duprey, Tonia Finnegan, Deborah L. Frederick, Alice Heckard, Natalie LeDuc, Michelle Menard, Devi Momot, Kristina Parker-Wingler, Vickie Phaneuf, Joyce Rafferty and Victoria Zinser Johnson.

In 2007, the Hudson Valley, Mohawk Pathways, Adirondack and North Country Girl Scout Councils joined together to create the Girl Scouts of Northeastern New York (GSNENY). With that change, the GSNENY services more than ten thousand girls and their families and numbers more than five thousand adults and volunteers.

SERVICE AND SOCIAL ORGANIZATIONS

Each of the women honored by the GSNENY shows traits that distinguish them from their peers, both in their work and in their other service to the community. They are not alone in those actions, however. Among the many women from Clinton County who have served willingly are those who belong to various other service organizations. It would be impossible to list all of those women on these pages, but a sampling shows the widespread dedication to good works.

Helen Isabel Smith serves as one example of wholehearted support of the community. Indeed, the *Plattsburgh Daily Press*, on September 14, 1918, remembered her by writing, "It is safe to say that no movement for the

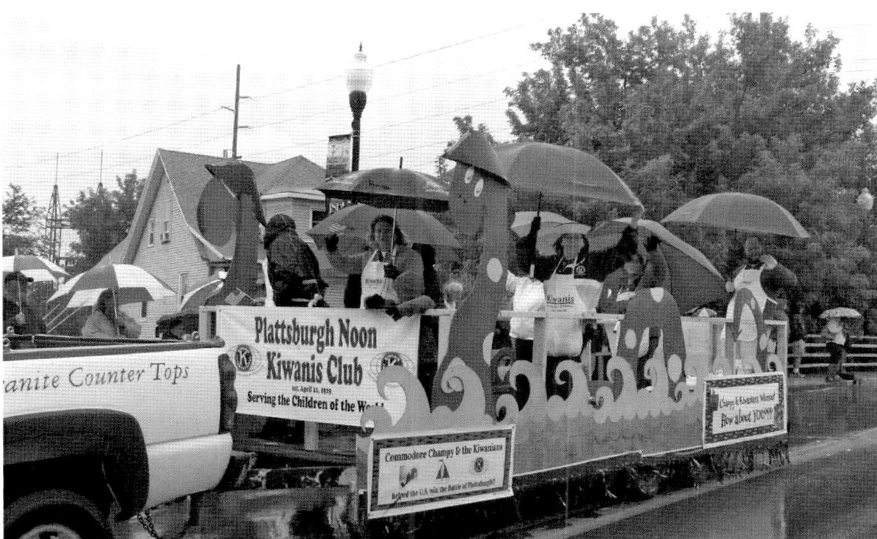

Nancy Church (middle) and the Plattsburgh Noon Kiwanis, one of several service organizations, at the 2014 Battle of Plattsburgh parade. *Nancy Church.*

betterment of conditions in our city has been started within the memory of her contemporaries that has not had her hearty co-operation." She was elected president of the Women's Auxiliary of the Champlain Valley Hospital, a post in which she served until illness forced her to stop a few days before her death. Smith also took a "lively interest in the Industrial school which for several sessions gathered one hundred and more little girls into its classes and taught the useful art of sewing while at the same time replenishing the wardrobes of the small pupils." Further, prior to the arrival of the Humane Society in the region, she "tried to secure for Plattsburgh a Branch Society for the Preservation of Cruelty to Animals. Failing in that, she kept a vigilant eye upon all cases of cruelty to her dear, dumb friends, and, aided by the police, who knew that her warm sympathy was seasoned with excellent commonsense, she saved not a few from abuse."

Another exemplar of community support was Dorothy Bourne Booth. Married to Alan Booth and the mother of three, Dorothy volunteered as a Girl Scout leader and board member. She also served on the United Way's Community Chest; the Clinton County Christmas Bureau, which she organized and co-chaired for sixteen years; the Children's Home, of which she was president for two years and a long-term board member; the Presbyterian Women's Association; the Children's Service committee; the County Mental Health Service Committee; the Joint Council on Economic Opportunity Committee; and the Plattsburgh Housing Committee. In 1971, she became the first woman in Clinton County to win the Law Day Liberty Bell Award, which recognizes a person or group who encourages greater respect for the rule of law and promotes civic responsibility in the community. The next year, she won the Clinton County Youth Bureau Award, which was followed by the Chamber of Commerce Service Award in 1974 and the Christmas Bureau Award in 1974. She was further honored by a Girl Scout flower garden in her memory and by the United Way's first annual award, which went to Dorothy and her husband in 1985 and was renamed the Dorothy and Alan Booth Distinguished Citizen of the Year Award in 1992. Writing of her activities in 1998 for a city of Plattsburgh project to commemorate the 150th anniversary of the Seneca Falls Convention, Alan explained, "Dorothy started volunteer activities when in college. She was always interested in the development and education of our youth and in helping people in need. Her primary interest was her own family but once her children were college bound Dorothy devoted her time to community activities. Dorothy was an optimist who always believed that community problems could and would be solved." Lee Lapensohn, in the *Press-Republican's*

"Editor's Corner," described her as having the "energy of a steam roller and very often in her zealous efforts to make true Christian charity a way of life, the impact as well." Continuing, she wrote, "Dorothy Booth has so many hats of goodness that one doesn't know where to start appropriately to cite her." Yet Booth's humility called her to "say it's the hundreds of other people and organizations working together that has brought to fruition the dreams of those who afford the luxuries of time, money and inclination as they think of helping their fellow man."

Similarly, Helen Wilcox Ianelli is noted for her community service. With roots in Plattsburgh dating back to the early nineteenth century, Helen graduated from Plattsburgh High school in 1947 and then began working for the New York Telephone Company. After being transferred to Rochester, she met and married John Ianelli; they, and the first two of their children, moved back to Plattsburgh in 1955, after which Helen opened the Jack and Jill Center, the first private and state-licensed nursery school in the area. From 1968 until 1975, she worked at St. John's Elementary School as an art teacher. When her husband entered the political arena, Helen's work in the community changed. She took over a not-for-profit organization called Plattsburgh Pride, the purpose of which was to support, in general, the larger community and, specifically, the city of Plattsburgh. She also started a bimonthly magazine called *Plattsburgh Alive.* Helen organized a guide service called Northeast Discoveries and developed a visitor's map titled *Discover Historic Plattsburgh*. Among the many groups who have benefited from her efforts are the Saranac Chapter Daughters of the American Republic, the Alice T. Miner Colonial Collection, the Kent-Delord House Garden Club, the North Country Cultural Center for the Arts and the Clinton Community College Foundation Board, of which she was president for four years. In 1979, Helen was named Business Woman of the Year by the Plattsburgh Business and Professional Women. She has also been recognized with the Boy Scouts' Distinguished Citizen Award (1993), the City of Plattsburgh's Volunteer of the Year (1993), the Council on the Arts for Clinton County's Annual Art Award (1994), the Kiwanis Club's Citizen of the Year Award (1995) and the Clinton-Essex-Franklin Library's Richard Lawrence Award (2000). Helen and her husband were also honored as the Chamber of Commerce's Irish Persons of the Year in 1987. In 2002, the *Press-Republican* issued a congratulations for her work, writing:

> *CHEERS: to Helen Ianelli for founding and then coordinating for over 18 years the annual sand-sculpture contest, Sunbeams of the Beach,*

which has been sponsored by the Press-Republican for the past decade. Besides registering, participating and choosing judges, Helen—a former art teacher—makes signs, judging sheets and numbers flags. She also sends thank-you notes to volunteers and even packs a picnic basket with lunch for the volunteers and brownies for the judges. As the wife of the mayor at the time, John Ianelli, Helen was extremely active with beautification projects and generally trying to make Plattsburgh a better place to live. The contest was an outgrowth of that drive. She has also been one of the Plattsburgh Public Library's greatest assets, coaxing activism and concern for another of the city's sometimes-undervalued jewels. She has charmed volunteers and participants for years. Her work's much appreciated.

POLITICS AND GOVERNMENT

Women have also served in the political and governmental arenas. One of the most famous of these women was Luella Robinson North, the daughter of Thomas Robinson, a Republican lawyer and an elected New York State assemblyman and senator, and Sarah Barber, a minister's daughter. Luella married Dr. Charles Henry North in 1900, and the couple moved to Dannemora, where Dr. North served as superintendent of the Dannemora State Hospital. While in Dannemora, Luella met women organizing a local chapter of the League of Women voters, occasionally entertaining them for tea, and was active in the Red Cross and in activities at the Plattsburgh Barracks during World War I. On December 12, 1917, Charles was killed by an inmate at the hospital, and his family members' lives changed immeasurably.

Four years later, after moving to Plattsburgh and assuming all of the household responsibilities that had previously fallen to staff members, Luella was approached by the Honorable John R. O'Brien, the Republican "boss" of Clinton County. Her daughter explains that O'Brien asked North to run for the newly created office of the Children's Court, telling her that she "would have jurisdiction over both delinquent children as well as those adjudged neglected. He also assured her that her duties would be light, only fifteen or twenty cases a year. He was certainly wrong about that!" A close personal friend of Carrie Chapman Catt, who founded the League of Women Voters, and member of a family that had long advocated education after high school for women so that they would be able to support themselves, Luella North was elected and then reelected to the position of

Children's Court judge of Clinton County, beginning her service at the age of fifty. North's daughter, Luella North Kimble, believed that her mother was "a natural campaigner" who "stressed the importance of family, and her concern for neglected youngsters. She firmly believed that delinquency was the result of poor parental guidance, but she also realized that real poverty made supervision of children difficult."

Penelope Clute also served as a jurist within Clinton County. Her legal career started in 1968, when she worked as a paralegal investigator for the Volunteers in Service to American Program (VISTA) at the Mandel Legal Aid Clinic, University of Chicago Law School. Later, as a student at Wayne State University Law School, she worked on the Release on Recognizance Program through the Detroit Recorder's Court (1971), served as the assistant to Olga Madar, vice president of the United Auto Workers (1971–72), and clerked for the Office of the University Attorney (1972–73). Upon graduation, Clute served as a staff attorney for the Center for the Administration of Justice at Wayne State University (1973–76) and as a hearings administrator for the Michigan Department of Corrections (1976–78). After her 1978 move to Plattsburgh, Penny and her partners opened Clute, Clute and Thompson. In that capacity, she contracted with Clinton County to offer legal assistance to senior citizens through the Office for the Aging. Her particular specialty, as listed in an October 17, 1980 *Press-Republican* article, was to "provide services in the field of administration law, which is expected to include the resolution of problems involving various government programs such as Social Security, Supplemental Security Income, and state and federal health programs."

Clute first expressed interest in running for the position of Clinton County district attorney in 1985, winning the Democratic nomination but ultimately losing to Andrew Ryan by a very narrow margin. When Ryan won a seat on the State Supreme Court in District Four, Governor Mario Cuomo appointed Clute the district attorney on January 1, 1989. She later ran on the Democratic ticket, winning reelection and serving in that capacity until December 2001. In 2002, she received a ten-year appointment as the Plattsburgh City court judge by Mayor Dan Stewart. During her time on the bench, Joe LoTemplio explains that Penelope Clute "implemented innovative and revolutionary programs to serve the people of Clinton County," programs that include a special focus on alternative sentencing methods for defendants with mental health or substance abuse issues and on the Clinton County Youth Court, serving on the Youth Court's advisory board from its beginning. That court focuses on youthful offenders committing first-time, minor offenses like shoplifting, criminal mischief and vandalism, letting the youth be defended, prosecuted and judged by his/her peers. Sentences include community-service hours, peer-pressure classes and mandatory service on at least one youth court jury.

For these varied services, Penny Clute was awarded the Behavioral Health Services North's Margaret Platt Community Service Award in 2005 and the National Alliance for Mental Health Advocate of the Year Award in 2006. In addition to her legal publications, she has also shown a great interest in local history. In 2005, she wrote about "The Plattsburgh Idea," in which Major General Leonard Wood proposed citizens' military training camps to prepare them for potential service in wartime, for *New York Archives*. She also wrote about Peggy Facto, the first woman executed in New York State. Facto, with Francis Labare, was indicted for killing her illegitimate baby. The indictment charged that the duo "as soon as the said infant was born with force and arms…being alive then and there being in the peace of god… feloniously, willfully and with malice aforethought did make an assault…and did take a certain string…of the bredth of one inch and of the length of two feet…and….so being fixed drawn and tied around the neck of the said child…did choke and strangle…and did cast throw and push into a certain place then and there situate wherein there was a great quantity of fire and… the said infant child by the fire was then and there burned to death and killed roasted and part consumed…and there instantly died." Though Facto testified against Labare, asserting that he killed the child on his own, she was found guilty and sentenced to death. In his denial of clemency, Governor Clinton stated that "the representation of the Judge and the facts of the case clearly establish the guilt of the convict and the horrible crime of infanticide evinces the necessity of penal influence."

Many other women have served in various governmental capacities. For example, several women across the country served as tax collectors. Margaret Ann Perry Bissonnette was elected tax collector for the village of Dannemora in 1927. Educated at the Sallaz Academy, which was staffed by the Sisters of St. Louis, and then at a district public school, Bissonnette was a substitute teacher at the Chazy Lake School in 1924 and 1925. She served as tax collector, school tax collector and clerk-treasurer of the village until the 1950s, "in spite of a progressive condition which began in the early 1930s and affected the use of her hands, arms and legs." From 1967 until 1985, Dora Young Rubado served as tax collector for the town of Ellenburg; she also served briefly as the town historian and, from 1965 until her retirement in 1984, worked in the Clinton County clerk's office. Other tax collectors have included Maud Ellenwood Perry Hilliard, Angeline Gervais, Mary

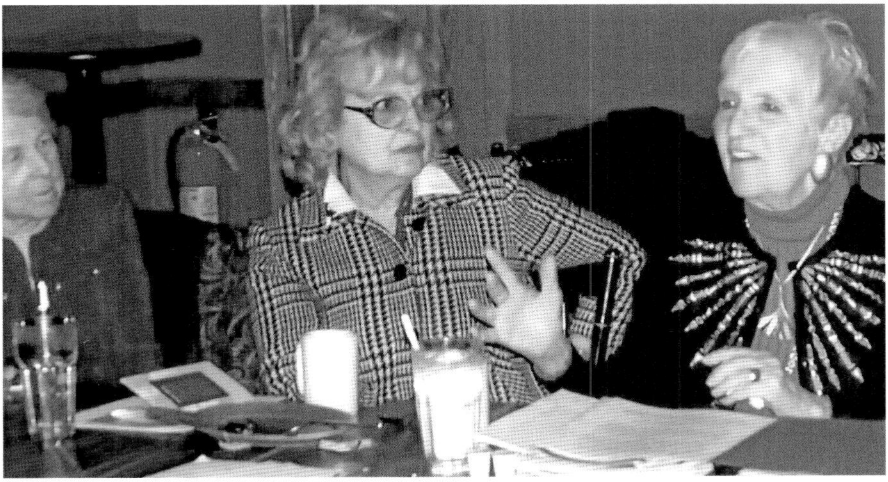

Sally Sears-Mack (right) addresses the Plattsburgh League of Women Voters, 2010. *Clinton County Historian's Office.*

Conners, Loretta Rushford, Sandra Spence, Beulah Hogle, Anna Mae Sorrell, Nettie Rabideau, Rose Barber, Margaret Goodrow, Beatrice Bosley, Dianne Goddeau, Bertha Rabideau, Helen O'Brien, Jean Craig, Julia Keysor, Bertha Wrisley, Florence Corron, Joan Tetreault, Shirley Gadway, Betty Favreau, Mary Bingel, Judith Cayea and Cornelia McPherson.

Others were town clerks, helping to conduct the business of their municipalities. June Coolidge Hinds served as the town of Ellenburg clerk from 1936 until 1955. A member of the Ellenburg Democratic Party, June also served as secretary of the Ellenburg Riverside Cemetery Association and was a member of the Ellenburg Depot Wesleyan Church. Helen Smith Soden followed as town clerk, serving from 1956 until 1962. During her tenure, Soden used her house as her office and held town meetings there. In addition to her work as clerk, Helen worked as a bookkeeper for S.L. Drown, McGregor's Hardware and the CVPH Medical Center. She was also active in various church organizations and in the Order of the Eastern Star. Town clerks have included Vivian Yelle, Margaret Goodrow, Audrey Trombly, Madelin Pombrio, Dana Donahue, Ida Grace Trumbell, Emma O'Brien, Nell Sullivan, Cassie Dame, Helen Smith, Vivian Yelle, Thelma LaBombard, Karlene Clark, Evelyn McNeil, Shirley Balko, Clara Bulriss Porter and Joanne Stafford.

Helen Carpenter Blow, born in Ellenburg Center, graduated from the Ellenburg High School and then from the Plattsburgh Normal School in

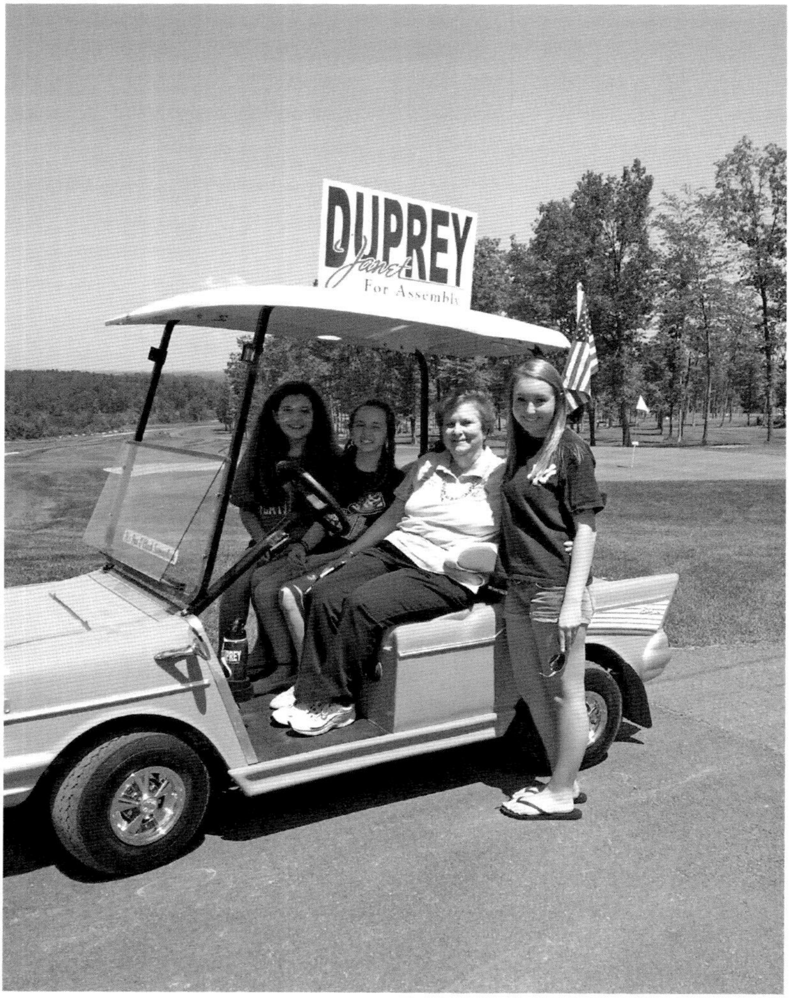

Janet Duprey and two of her granddaughters on the golf course and campaign trail. *Michelle Duprey Timmons.*

1933. She taught in a rural, one-room schoolhouse in Ellenburg Center for nine years and then at Ellenburg Central School for two years. In November 1946, she started to work at the Clinton County Department of Social Services, where she was a caseworker for five years. After then serving as an intake worker, Helen was promoted to supervisor. She retired as the director of Social Services in 1979, when she also received the Distinguished Service Award and the Community Service Award.

Included among the women who have worked in various non-elected governmental positions are Anna Neely, Dorothy Trombley, Frances Peryea, Claire Pulrang, Laurie Provoncha Kelso, Bertha Desjardins, Mary Fortin, Julie Dowd, Jeanine Leggett, Kunigunde Mueller, Margaret Giam-Bruno, Ruth Winter, Jeannine Bell, Kathy Brown, Melodie Lemieux, Kimberly Currier, Christie Drake, Jennifer Belli, Lois McShane, Bonnie Fenwick, Judy Kieslich and Barbara Foster.

One of the most famous Clinton County women in politics and government is Janet Duprey. A lifelong resident of Peru, Janet is first a wife, mother and grandmother. But she is also an active politician who has achieved great things. The first woman elected to the Clinton County legislature (1976), Janet served five two-year terms on the legislature. During her tenure, she served on all nine standing committees, chaired the Ways and Means (Finance) Committee in 1983 and the Human Services Committee for seven years and was the chairperson of the legislature in 1981 and 1982. After completing her service as legislator, Janet was elected Clinton County treasurer, a position she held from 1986 until 2006, when she ran for and was elected to the New York State Assembly. Active in the Clinton County Republican Party, she simultaneously served on a variety of party committees and was the 2004 alternate delegate to the Republican National Convention.

Behind the scenes of her political career, Janet Duprey is active within the community. Among the groups with whom she works are Apple Valley Senior Housing in Peru, the CVPH Medical Center, the Clinton Community College and SUNY Plattsburgh Nursing Advisory Committees, Hospice of the North Country, the American Red Cross–North Country Chapter, Pine Harbour Assisted Living & Memory Care Center, Champlain Valley Business and Professional Women and the League of Women Voters. She also works with SUNY Plattsburgh's Spectrum Advisory Committee, literally wearing her support—in the form of a blue puzzle piece used as the symbol of autism awareness—in virtually every public appearance. Understandably, that work has garnered attention and awards. The Clinton County Business and Professional Women named her Woman of the Year in 1984. She was also named New York State County Finance Official of the Year in 2004 and a Girl Scout Woman of Distinction in 2008. During 2011, she received the State of Vermont BPW Alice Paul Award and the Behavioral Health Services North Community Service Award. Finally, in 2012, she was named to the Advocacy and Resource Center Wall of Fame. Janet's political career and community service have tied her firmly to the North Country and to

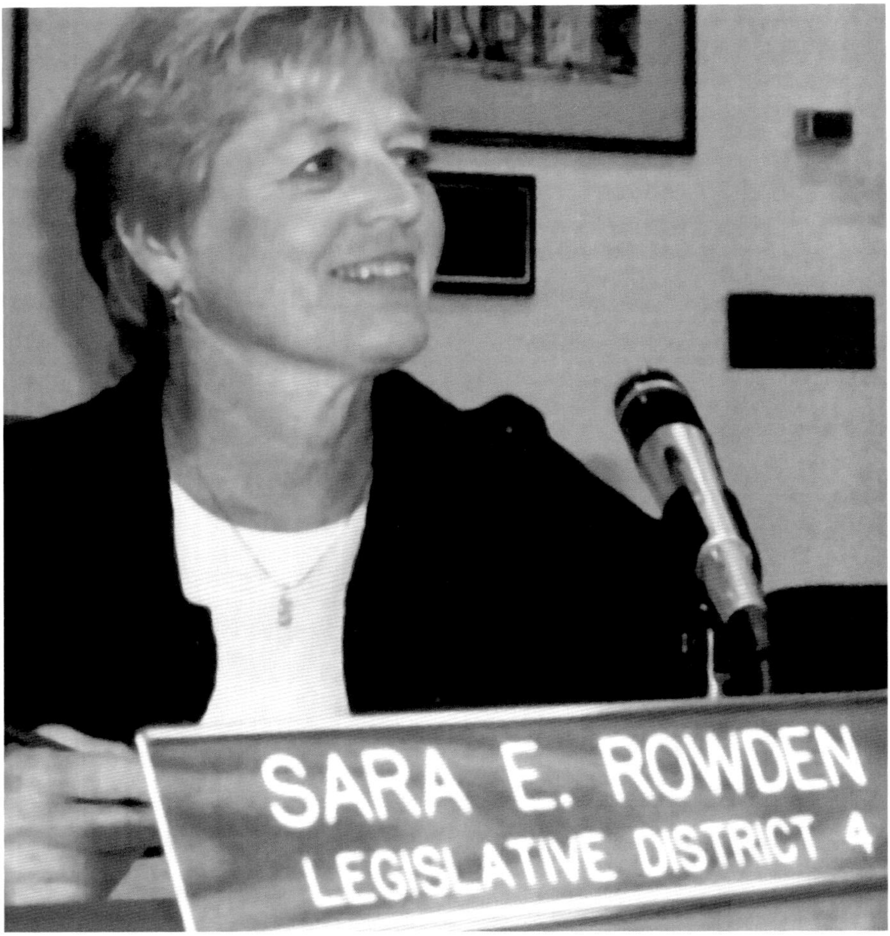

Sara Rowden, a Democrat, who served as legislator for Area 4. *Clinton County Historian's Office.*

other women whose service and philanthropy started the very organizations that later honored her.

Women active in local politics have included Margaret Coolaw, Bernadette Nichols, Frada Santimore, Sharon LaFave, Gloria Ryan, Nancy McGaulley, Irene LaValley, Ruth Snyder, Irene Gero, Katherine Kelley, Ethel DeCoste, Marguerite Tamer, Susan Castine, Rose Marie Miller, Florence Corron, Candis Luck, Ethel Stewart, Martha Sweeney, Judith Rule, Shirley Durnin, Beverly Lamberton, Rita Humphrey, Nancy DuFrain, Mary Gilmore, Cynthia Sample, Martha Sweeney, Mary Fowler, Gladys Perry, Christine Rotella, Cassie Dame, Maureen Brewster, Celine Paquette, Melissa Penfield,

Shirley Thomas, Barbara LaDuke, Hilda Danforth, Ellen Montgomery, Janice Letourneau, Donna LaMare, Michelle Tolosky, Melissa McManus, Sarah Rowden, Christine Bezrutczyk, Rachelle Armstrong, Becky Kasper, Kimberly Davis and Patty Waldron.

PHILANTHROPY

One of the most recognizable institutions in Clinton County is the Vilas Home, an adult home for senior citizens that celebrated its 125th anniversary in 2012. Originally called the S.F. Vilas Home for Aged and Infirm Women, the home was established by Harriet Hunt Vilas in memory of her late husband. With a gift of $50,000, of which half was dedicated to the building and half to an endowment fund, Vilas planned the building with the architect, Marcus F. Cummings. Situated on a parcel of land donated by heirs of the Vilas estate, the home included forty-five rooms.

When the *Plattsburgh Sentinel* published its *Souvenir Industrial Edition of Plattsburgh 1897*, the Vilas Home had five residents. An 1891 visitor to the home, Mrs. Haskell, of Chazy, donated $20,000 to the endowment. The publisher elaborated on this project, saying, "Mrs. Vilas' gift has been

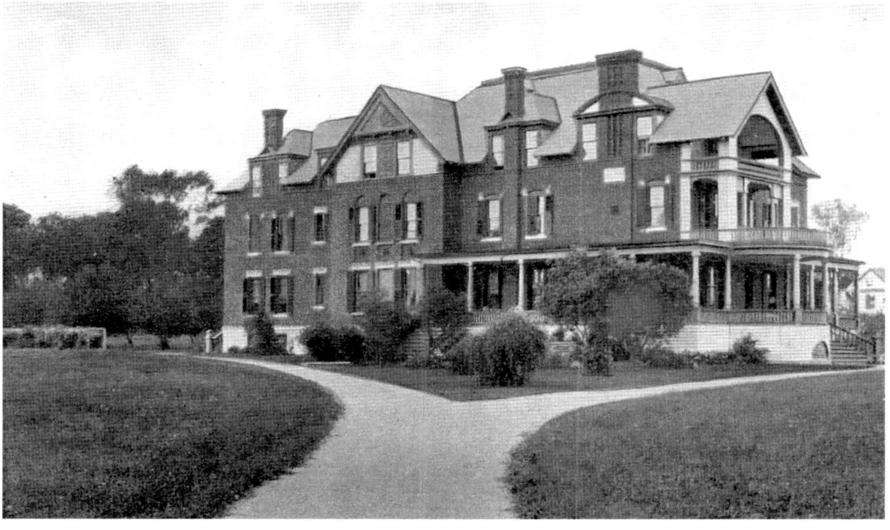

The Samuel F. Vilas Home, on the corner of Beekman and Margaret Streets in Plattsburgh. *Clinton County Historian's Office.*

referred to as a charity, but it is not such a charity as in any sense humiliates and degrades the recipient, but that kind, considerate, womanly charity, which simply holds out a helping hand to an aged sister and equal. It is that kind of charity which relieves aged ladies of some of the wants and cares sometimes put upon the noblest and best of women in their old age. It is a charity which makes the declining years of their lives more pleasant. Mrs. Vilas has extended her mantel of benevolence over other counties—Clinton, Essex, and Franklin." In its November 3, 1899 edition, the *Plattsburgh Sentinel* described her funeral, conducted by Reverend Joseph Gamble and Reverend A.H. Easton at the First Presbyterian Church, thus: "All in the audience felt as though a friend and chief benefactor had gone from Plattsburgh in the person of the gentle, gracious woman who lay in the casket literally covered with flowers. Among the mourners who followed her to her last resting place in Riverside Cemetery were the inmates of the Vilas Home able to be present, to whom her grand gift is a benefaction."

WOMEN'S CHRISTIAN TEMPERANCE UNION (WCTU)

Founded in 1874 in Cleveland, Ohio, the Women's Christian Temperance Union (WCTU) worked to convince Americans that abstaining from alcohol was morally, ethically and medically important. Through its work, the WCTU intended to protect the home, offering a slogan, "For God and Home and Native Land," which was later changed to "For God and Home and Every Land." The organization was arranged nationally, with local chapters connected to state unions and the national headquarters. When Frances Willard became the national president of the WCTU in 1879, she adopted a policy of complete reform, believing that use of alcohol, drugs and tobacco was symptomatic of society's larger problems. Included in that policy of reform were endorsements of women's suffrage. In fact, the organization has lasted into the present through its work with women. The organization, on its website, explains, "Today the WCTU is the oldest voluntary, non-sectarian woman's organization in continuous existence in the world. The WCTU is a founding member (1888) of the National Council for Women (Frances Willard was its first president) and the International Council of Women in 1893. It is also a charter member (1945) of the United Nations Non-Governmental Organizations (NGO). For almost 125 years the WCTU has trained women to think on their feet, speak in public, and run an organization."

From its original platform of abstinence, the group has moved on to protecting women and children at home and work, establishing shelters for abused women and children, advocating for an eight-hour workday plus equal pay for equal work, founding kindergartens, assisting in the creation of parent-teacher associations, supporting federal aid for education, seeking stiffer penalties for sexual crimes and uniform marriage and divorce laws, requiring prison reform as well as female police officers and prison matrons, promoting nutrition and the pure food and drug act, offering legal aid, assisting in passive demonstrations, supporting laborers' right to organize and most generally promoting world peace.

In Clinton County, the WCTU was active throughout the twentieth century. Perhaps the most famous of the group's local members was Frances "Fanny" Hall, granddaughter of Henry and Elizabeth Delord. Fanny, who was married to the Reverend Francis Hall, served as the secretary of the Plattsburgh Union of the WCTU, which formed in 1874. Later, as the movement gained traction in the region, the *Plattsburgh Sentinel* gave the group a weekly column. By 1890, ten more WCTU unions existed in the county. They held regular meetings and conventions in Beekmantown, Champlain, Perry's Mills, Plattsburgh and beyond, inviting speakers like Emma Willard and PA Burdick to attend and offer lectures for the membership. Allan Everest explains that they also "publicly attacked the sellers of alcoholic beverages and conducted an intensive educational campaign through the Sunday schools." Fanny Hall was quite dedicated to the movement, forbidding wine to be served at communion in her husband's church, compiling a large library of temperance materials and serving as a speaker for the group. Actually, she served as the county's representative at state conventions for twenty-five years and attended national conferences, as well. Although she opposed the association of the New York State WCTU with a political party in 1885, she remained active in the association, as president of the county WCTU, until her later years. Of the fruits of her labor, historian Allan Everest wrote, "Her work, and that of others like her, may help to explain why Plattsburgh adopted citywide prohibition in 1918, two years before national prohibition went into effect."

Fanny's activism was not confined to the WCTU, though. Indeed, she worked on the Relief Committee of the Ladies' Relief Corps, a group that focused on the hardships experienced by women, and was one of the founders of the Home for the Friendless in Northern New York. That home, which was located on Broad Street, was created to "establish and maintain a house of industry for the relief of friendless, destitute or unprotected females, and for destitute or unprotected children," according to Allan Everest.

HOME FOR THE FRIENDLESS

A May 16, 1951 *Press-Republican* article celebrating the seventy-seventh anniversary of the home traces the facility's founding to Marcia Brown, principal of young women at the Plattsburgh Academy, who discovered a baby boy on a visit to the Clinton County Poor House and related the story of the child, "ill, scantily clothed, and cared for by idiotic women in a building she described as a 'miserable structure.'" Her story inspired a group of women, including Margaret Platt, a member of the family for whom Plattsburgh is named, to create the Home for the Friendless. Besides caring for orphaned and abandoned children, the home evolved to offer treatment, rehabilitation and support for anybody experiencing mental illness. With this change in purpose, the home became known as the Children's Home of Northern New York (1919) and later the Northern New York Center. In 1999, the Northern New York Center and the Mental Health Association of Clinton County—formed in 1963 to expand mental health services for children and adults throughout the county—merged to become Behavioral Health Services North.

Funded almost entirely by volunteer subscriptions and donations, the objective of the original Home for the Friendless, as restated in the *Souvenir Industrial Edition of 1897*, was "to maintain a house of industry and home for the relief of friendless and unprotected children. The by-laws also provide that friendless and destitute females, over three years of age, and boys over three and under ten, either orphans or abandoned by their parents, may be received and provided for until permanent homes in Christian families can be secured for them, by adoption or otherwise. All inmates of the institution, of sufficient age, are expected to appropriate a sufficient portion of their time to manual labor, while they remain, and to be under the control of the matron." The original members of the corporation were Margaret Platt, Catherine Frederika Bulkley, Deborah Bixby, Margaret Edwards, Hannah Lansing, Sarah Williams, Joanne Clark, Mary Foote, Margaret Palmer, Welthy Orvis, Frances Hall, Charlotte Norton and Margaret Myers. After incorporation by the New York state legislature on May 20, 1874, the facility opened in a small house at the head of Broad Street, in a premises donated by M.K. Platt. Later moves brought the facility to Oak Street (1877) and Broad Street (1892), at which time all of the general officers of the home were women, as were the matron of the facility, the director of the educational department and two caretakers who helped clean and maintain a two-story building described as "well equipped for the purposes for which it was established" and built at a cost of about $12,000. Among the features of the building were a kitchen, pantries, storerooms, a dining room and a laundry in the basement; a matron's room, a parlor, play rooms and bathrooms on the first floor; a hospital, a nursery, a teacher's room, caretakers' rooms and three dormitories for girls on the second floor; and three dormitories for boys on the third floor, presumably an attic floor. Others who worked at the home included Miss Arnold (teacher), Hannah Ellenwood (teacher), Miss DeLong (matron, 1908) and Ellen Scully, whose tombstone in Riverside Cemetery explains that "she was an assistant Matron at the/Home, a faithful conscientious Christian; beloved and respected by all who knew her." Later, in 1912, the home moved to the renovated Palmer House on Bailey Avenue, adding a wing to the east side of the structure to serve as a dormitory for the boys and a small building at the rear to serve as an infirmary; a further dormitory addition was built in 1924, allowing the home to serve up to forty children. In 1951, those running the home were happy to announce in a May 16 *Plattsburgh Press-Republican* article that "throughout the years, the ideals of the founders have been realized because of the devoted work and generosity of countless helpers. A homelike atmosphere has always been emphasized, as well as the highest standards of health and safety. Contributions to the Community Chest in Plattsburgh and memberships from out of town residents permit continuation of the work this year, as do gifts of food, clothing, toys, games, and many services performed without charge. Parties, picnics, movies and trips arranged by friends of the children help to make it truly a home." Currently, BHSN, a locally owned and operated not-for-profit, maintains more than twenty sites and operates under a fifteen-member board of directors.

Another local group that serves those with brain disorders of all types and offers support for their families is the National Alliance on Mental Health–Champlain Valley chapter. The group provides education, advocacy and other services. Several women were instrumental in establishing and maintaining this group. They include Terri Winterbottom, Anne Bailey, Marguerite Adelman, Carrie Levessaur, Eveylne Tropper, Theresa Bennett and Amanda Bulris.

REFUGEES

A different type of service to those in need occurred locally when an increase in refugees to Canada prompted increased clearance procedures for entry to the country. In 1987, refugees started arriving in Plattsburgh, which "became a lifeline for the world's homeless." The number of refugees and the need for assistance was great, which prompted Brian Smith (director of the Plattsburgh Community Crisis Center), Jeanie Roberts (director of the American Red Cross in Plattsburgh) and Rose Pandozy (commissioner of Clinton County Social Services) to meet weekly and to call for help from the community at large. Among the women who answered the call, helping with everything from transporting refugees to and from doctor's appointments, preparing and delivering food, raising money, translating documents and conversations, finding housing, staffing shelters, filling prescriptions, serving as nurses and teaching the refugees, were Margot Zeglis (coordinator of volunteers at Catholic Charities), Kathy Champagne and Maureen Lynch (social services workers), Sue Stewart, Cindy Pytlak, Ginger (at the Salvation Army), Nancy Tyrell (staff member at the Salvation Army), Sister Monique (regional director of the Department of Christian Formation for the Diocese of Ogdensburg at Plattsburgh), Pat Cote, Rosemary McNamara, Meredith O'Connor (art teacher), Captain Kathy Douglas (Salvation Army), Rita Jolicoeur (Retired Senior Volunteer Program), Margaret Erno, Delia Trombley, Bev Frasier, Ann Allen and Sister Theresa Moan (teachers at OLV Secretarial School) and members of the United Methodist Women.

As a result of this refugee work, another local service project was born. Sister Debbie Blow, honored as a NYS Senate Woman of Distinction in 2013 because of this work, first met the Flores family when they escaped the social unrest of their native Nicaragua. According to an article by Katherine Clark titled "Area Women Help," Sister Debbie "helped provide the family with a small apartment that was donated by a local landlord, all furniture and beds, food for several weeks, clothing for the entire family, contacts for employment, and education for their two children." Then, after Hurricane Mitch devastated Nicaragua in 1998, Sister Debbie and the Flores family took action. Over the course of the year, fifty-two volunteers traveled to Nicaragua to provide health care, construction work, education and other services. Among those who volunteered were Eve McGill and Yamilette Flores, who, as emissaries of Seton Catholic School, went to Nicaragua and distributed goods, including ten blankets sent by the Champlain Valley Quilters' Guild, and money to people in need. According to Suzanne

Moore, "From North Country donations, McGill and Flores gave money for a library building and to bring electricity to the elementary classrooms. They left tuition of $100 for each of 10 youngsters." They also provided $4,000 to build two single-family homes that had been washed away by flooding.

ALICE T. MINER

Another philanthropist of note was Alice Trainer, who married William H. Miner in 1895. She is most remembered for her museum, the Alice T. Miner Museum, a colonial revival museum, though her good works are not limited to that institution. Indeed, Miner hosted many parties at her home, Heart's Delight Farm, to benefit the Physicians Hospital, the Red Cross and the families of her employees. With her husband, who made his fortune selling patented railroad devices, she was committed, according to the museum website's welcome page, "to improving the economy, education, and culture of the Chazy area, where William, as a young orphan, had worked on his Uncle John's farm." In addition to the local school, the Miners built a model farm, a series of dams, several buildings and, perhaps most significantly, the Physicians Hospital in Plattsburgh. On her death in 1950, Alice was remembered as having been "active in the work of the various institutions which Mr. Miner sponsored and to which he contributed so much during his lifetime. She was most generous in her contributions to these institutions as well as to many other charitable organizations." Among other things, she served as the vice-president and director of the Physicians Hospital, vice-president of the Women's League of the hospital, vice-president and director of the Kent-Delord House Museum, president of the board of education of the Chazy Central Rural School, president of the Alice T. Miner Colonial Collection, chairman of the board of directors of W.H. Miner, Inc., and a trustee of the William H. Miner Foundation. Her obituary continues to explain that "the passing of Mrs. Miner marks the close of a chapter of exceptional progress in the development of charitable and educational institutions in Clinton County, made possible by her and her husband, during the past half century."

Miner's generosity and charity continued after her death, with the bequests and trusts she established in her will. Beyond her family and friends, legacies were left for the employees of the Heart's Delight Cottage and Heart's Delight Farm, and seven trusts were established for the Presbyterian and

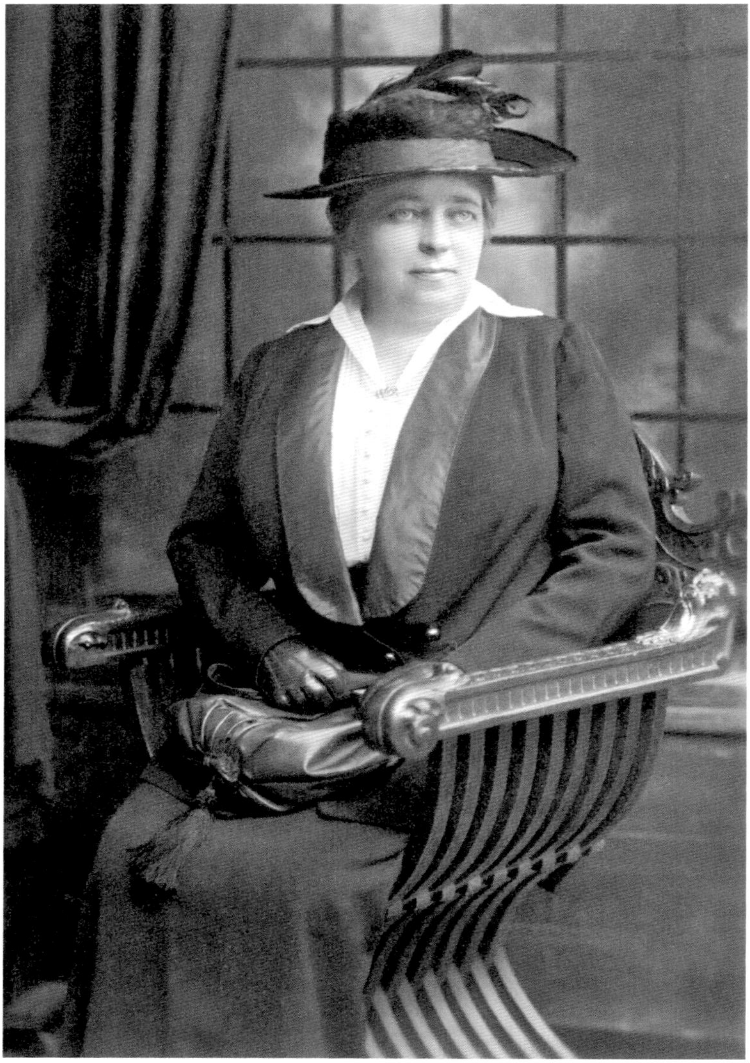

Alice T. Miner, founder of a local history museum and local philanthropist. *Alice T. Miner Colonial House Museum.*

Congregational Church and Society at Chazy, the Chazy Riverside Cemetery, the maintenance and preservation of memorial windows for the Miners at the Presbyterian Church, the Children's Home of Northern New York, the Physicians Hospital (which now recognizes her philanthropy with its Alice T. Miner Center for Women and Children) and the Alice T. Miner Colonial

Collection. Joseph Burke, who was quoted in a summer 2013 *All Points North* article, explains that the collection, which includes items that Alice began gathering in 1910, "offers a unique entrée to her heart, head, and hopes—the place to find her taste, temperament, and talent." The museum opened in 1924 and has since served as a place for people to learn about eighteenth-century life. Over the years, a variety of directors and curators have worked within the museum. Most recently Amanda Palmer (2006–2014) and Ellen Adams have undertaken the job of protecting Mrs. Miner's collection and bringing local history to the wider world through tours of the facility, special programming, a website, a blog and social media pages.

Susan Spissinger has also served the community in a variety of ways. An active member of the board of directors of the Plattsburgh Memorial Chapel and a retired Plattsburgh State administrator, Spissinger offered an example of how a woman can succeed in the workplace while also maintaining a rewarding personal life. While managing a demanding yet fulfilling career and sharing domestic responsibilities for her home, she pursued a PhD. Because of her example as a Girl Scout leader, countless young girls learned that, through dedication, they could do anything. Another of the gifts that she gave to a generation of girls was an appreciation for this place. Among the

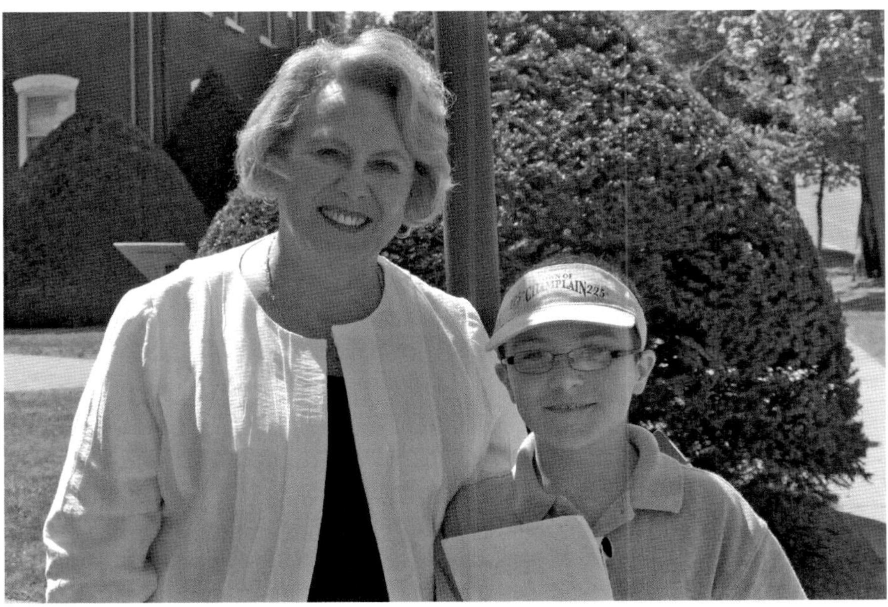

Celine Paquette, with her young historian friend, 2013. *Author's collection.*

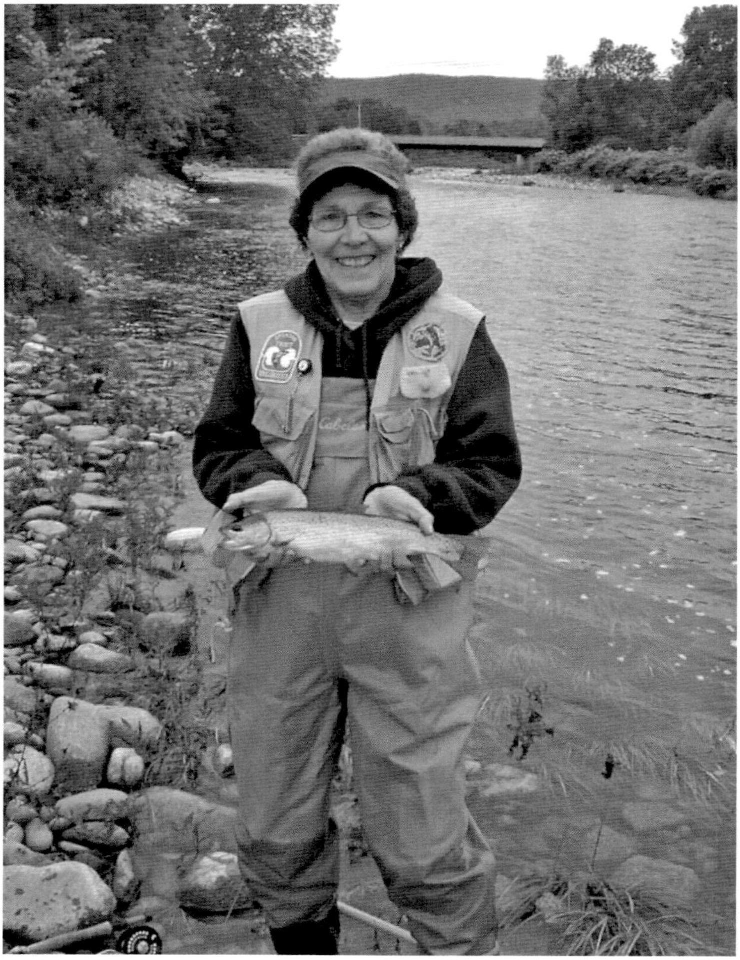

Susan Spissinger enjoying the great outdoors. *Jessica Spissinger.*

virtues she highlighted were the region's lakes, streams and mountains. But Sue also emphasized the beauty of everyday experiences, like mowing the lawn in a place where the air is clean. Fishing, skiing and hiking were among the various activities she has shared.

Others who have professed a love for Clinton County, the Adirondacks and the various outdoor experiences possible here are Jacqueline Gray, Janet Edwards, Amanda Bourcy, Karla Deyo, Doris Armstrong, Cecilia Coolidge, Geraldine Timosevich, Kathryn Lester, Joan Signor, Nancy Lewis, Irene Bezio, Elizabeth Chapman and Mildred Russell.

Chapter 5

BELIEF

Although the county is home to several denominations, the preponderance of people who profess some sort of religious belief makes clear that faith is important to women in this area. Whether through general statements of belief, specific profession of vows or membership in faith-based groups, women throughout the history of Clinton County have had active religious lives.

David Kellogg pointed out some of those beliefs in his journal, writing, in 1901, about a patient who "has been between life and death for a long time, but is much better now and will recover. She told me today that the doctors, her mother and prayers had saved her life. I have learned that she had made a vow to God that she will wear black all her life if He allows her to recover." Another local woman, Caroline Adriance Platt, was said to have "read and cherished her Dutch Bible throughout her life."

Frances Delord Webb was devout in her faith. Writing to her husband, Francis, in 1833, she said, "My Beloved Husband, How dear to my heart are your kind expressions of love. The hold you have upon my affections is deep, sacred and deathless. I sometimes fear that you are too much the idol of my heart, for we are taught to devote the first offering of our hearts unto God. But I would that you were altogether persuaded to be a Christian. Defer it no longer, dearest, for it concerns too highly your eternal welfare to be neglected." Upon her death, Webb was praised in the *Albany Journal and Telegraph* for her great belief: "While her conversation always indicated reflection and intelligence, there was not the semblance of affectation or pedantry, but an enlightened and fervent piety. She first made a profession of faith in Christ in the Episcopalian faith at the age of fifteen. Since when she has adorned the doctrine of God her Savior by a holy life."

Regardless of the specific tenets of their belief, women like Webb and Platt led to a strong religious life within the county, one that spanned specific denominations. The Order of the Eastern Star (OES) is perhaps the best example of that emphasis on religious belief regardless of denomination. Distantly related to the Freemasons, the OES "is a social order comprised of persons with spiritual values, but it is not a religion. Its appeal rests in the true beauty of the refreshing and character-building lessons that are so sincerely portrayed in its ritualistic work. A deep fraternal bond exists between its members. It is the wholesome relationship of sisterly and brotherly love brought about through high principles exemplified in our lives which makes us near and dear to each other." On its website, the group explains that its membership is "composed of people of deep spiritual convictions," adding that "it is open to all faiths, except no faith." Their stated goals are to develop and show charity, truth and loving kindness.

Clinton County has been home to several chapters of the OES, including the Cumberland Bay, Chazy, Dawn, Washington, Mount Herman, Prospect and Mooers Miramichi chapters. Each group arranged a variety of activities,

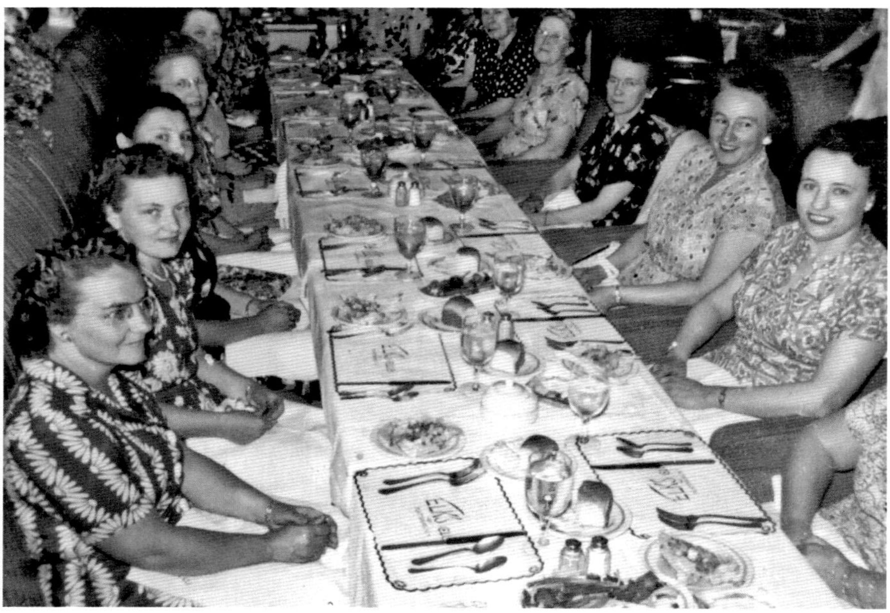

Members of the Ellenburg women's organization enjoy dinner together, 1950s. *Clinton County Historian's Office.*

including regular meetings, family picnics, banquets and dinners, often with the express purpose of raising money for charitable causes. The Mount Herman Chapter 653, which operates in Ellenburg and was described in *Ellenburg Yesterday and Today*, included "contributions to the charities of the Grand Chapter of New York including veterans, OES Home in Oriskany, elderly members in need and special emergency situations. Educational grants are given to members and their children for assistance in attending college."

Members of the OES tend to continue with the group throughout their lives. The Ellenburg group, for example, boasted eleven women who had belonged for more than fifty years: Grace Huggins (sixty-eight years), Mattie Cheeseman (sixty-seven years), Pauline Adams (sixty-five years), Eloise McGregor (sixty-three years), Florence Sunderland (sixty years), Lillian Patnode (sixty years), Josie Triggett (fifty-seven years), Florence Gibson (fifty-six years), Viola Baxter (fifty-six years), Adah Gilmore (fifty years) and Mildred Dominy (fifty years).

In 1921, Emma Chandler was honored for her service, with details of the ceremony provided in a November 20, 1975 *North Countryman* article. During her thirty-three years in the OES, she served as conductress, worthy matron, associate matron and musician. At the time of the dinner in honor of Emma and her husband, Charles, she served as treasurer, an office she had held for the last twenty-two years. Her colleagues said of her: "A fortune teller once told Emma years ago that she would handle a lot of money…but it would never be her own! Also in serving as musician, it was noted that she has served a long time 'on the bench.' Emma has always been an inspiration to others, always ready to give raise and lift up the morale of all. Her work in the Chapter has been unending. Always doing just a little bit more than what has been asked of her and really dedicated to her work, and a true and wonderful friend to every member."

Among the many other women who worked with the OES are Joyce Gordon, Bernyce Cook, Geraldine Welden, Ethel Sample, Viola White, Mildred York Rennell and Ruth Hardy.

DENOMINATIONAL WORSHIP

Moving into the realm of denominational faith, the name Georgia Harkness stands out as significant. Born in Harkness—a hamlet named for her family—Georgia studied at a one-room schoolhouse until she turned twelve and then

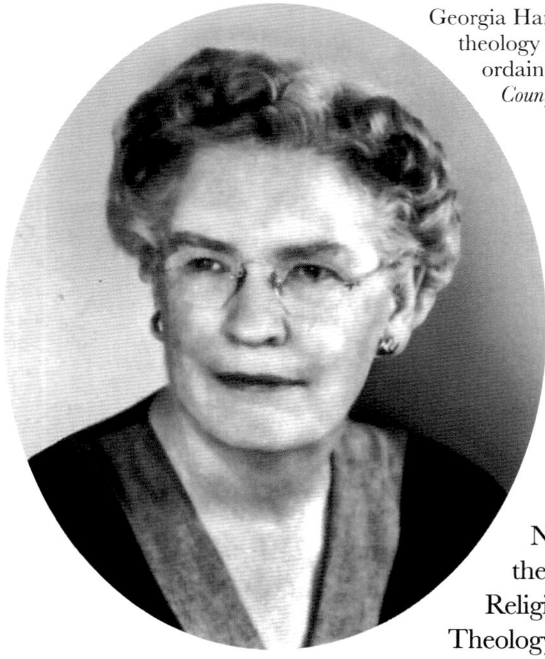

Georgia Harkness, who taught religion, theology and philosophy and was an ordained Methodist minister. *Clinton County Historian's Office.*

attended Keeseville High School, earning an honors diploma. She earned a state scholarship to attend Cornell University, from which she earned an AB and was elected Phi Beta Kappa. After teaching Latin and French in Schuylerville, New York, Harkness attended the Boston University School of Religious Education and School of Theology, earning an MA, an MRE and a PhD. Georgia used her degree to become the first woman in applied theology to be named a professor at a major seminary, teaching philosophy and religion at Elmira College, Mount Holyoke College, the Garret Biblical Institute, the Pacific School of Religion, Japan International Christian University and Union Theological Seminary of Manila.

The descendant of Quakers in Peru, Georgia Harkness was first ordained as a deacon in the Methodist Episcopal Church (Troy Conference) in 1926 and "was a long-time advocate of full status for women clergy within the church. She was given great credit for legislation eventually affecting it in 1956," when full membership was gained. In 1938, Harkness was appointed a local elder of the church. Over the course of her career, she wrote more than twenty books on religion and presented many theological lectures. She was granted honorary degrees in divinity, letters and the law and was named "one of the ablest of U.S. female divines" by *Time* magazine in 1938 and "Churchwoman of the Year" by the Religious Heritage of America, Inc., in 1958. Despite her many activities—which included serving as a U.S. representative to the international enclave in an effort to create a committee focused on world affairs—Georgia Harkness maintained a home in the hamlet of her birth throughout her life, returning for summer vacations and for various ceremonies to celebrate the history of the region.

Women were active in the creation of many Methodist churches in Clinton County, often serving as the earliest congregants. Ann Durkey, Mary Bacon, Maria Haynes, Polly Averill, Patience Miller, Philena Brock, Phebe Edgerton and Ann Smith were among them. Carrie Barrett and Mattie Booth were also noted for organizing the Plattsburgh Cadets, a group of girls that conducted drills on the lawns of the Andrew Williams home and in the Court Street theater.

More consistent service occurs through the United Methodist Women (UMW), an organization whose mission, according to the national organization's website, "is fostering spiritual growth, developing leaders and advocating for justice." First organized in 1869, when a meeting was held as a means of combatting the lack of women's health in India, the UMW included both missionary and ladies' aid societies, all of which focused on several core principles and values, promoting the empowerment of women, children and youth; anti-racism and multiculturalism; inclusion and equity; fair labor practices; and economic and environmental stewardship and sustainability. Their vision is to turn "faith, hope and love into action on behalf of women, children and youth around the world."

The UMW of Ellenburg, described in *Ellenburg Yesterday and Today*, shares that history. Before 1915, the Ladies' Aid Society was developed "to assist in caring for the church and raising money for the pastor's salary and other expenses." Later, around 1930, a Women's Home Missionary Society was founded. The two, eventually, merged with the Women's Society of

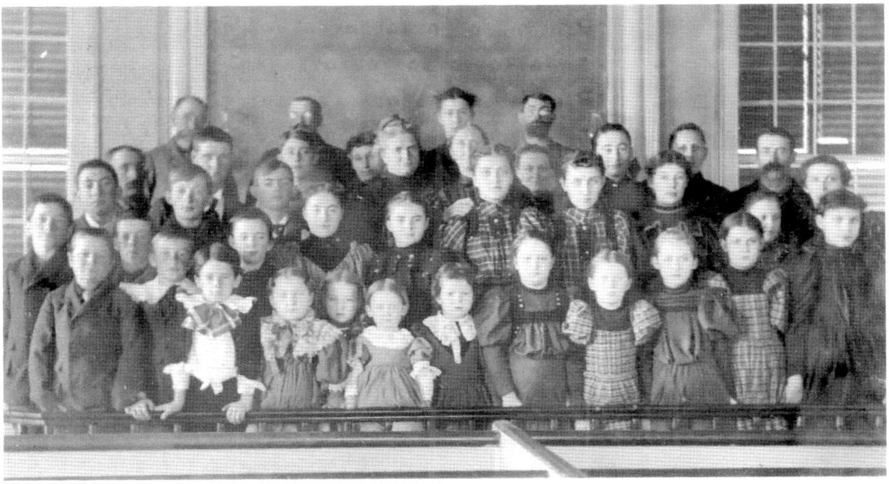

An unnamed group of Plattsburgh students and teachers. *Clinton County Historian's Office.*

Christian Service (1939) and the local establishment of the UMW (1972). One of the groups that came together to form this chapter of the UMW, the Friendly Circle, gathered fifteen to twenty women twice a month, "mixing social engagement with fancy work, which—along with jellies and pickles—was sold at a special Christmas sale, with money used for appliances and furniture for the parsonage."

Groups of UMW existed in Champlain, Chazy, Dannemora, Harkness, Keeseville, Lyon Mountain, Morrisonville, Peru, Plattsburgh, Saranac and Schuyler Falls. The Plattsburgh United Methodist Church's UMW meets monthly and, among other things, sponsors two large rummage sales to benefit Lenten Luncheons and the Henderson Settlement Mission. Similar fundraisers are undertaken by all of the women, who also come together in district and regional meetings to attend special presentations, discuss special church services and celebrations, plan fundraising efforts and engage in fellowship with one another. Pursuant to the group's mission, the UMW sponsors local programs as well. The October 2013 award of $15,000 to the Friends of the North Country, a not-for-profit housing and community development organization that operates in Clinton, Essex and Franklin Counties, for example, was intended to help women learn the financial tools necessary to be independent and successful.

Included among the local women who have been active in the UMW are Lorraine Smith, Marion Moore, Katherine Ohl Lewis, Mildred Dominy, Gladys Rubado, C. Frances Hobbs, Blanche Moore, Enid Daniels, Melba Cashman, Bertha Coolidge, Carrol Smith, Audrey Blow, Pauline Cashman, Kathleen Schumacher, Helen Blow, Mattie Cheeseman and Katherine Stafford Miller.

Others who have served their churches include Barbara Fry, who works alongside her husband at the Bible Baptist Church and leads their school; Dorothy "Dot" Crawford, who coordinates the Interfaith Council of Plattsburgh and Clinton County Food Shelf and won the United Way Volunteer of the Year Award in 2008; Marianne Wilson, who serves as the Director of Youth and Family Ministries at the First Presbyterian Church of Plattsburgh; the Reverend Dr. Patricia Schick, pastor of the First Presbyterian Church of Plattsburgh; Lori Sayah Kashorek, who devotes a great deal of time to the Church of Christ in Plattsburgh; Suzanne Van Arragon Spronk, who with her family and the assistance of the North Country Alliance Church, began a mission to support the Women and Children's Hospital in Mali, West Africa; Elisabeth Kevorkian, who, as the chairperson of the Lutheran Church of the Redeemer Care Team, leads visits to the ill, hospitalized or homebound; Becky

Poor, who is the senior pastor of the Saranac Community Church; Joceyln Erkenbeck, Patricia Martin, Shirley Germain and Lucinda Allen, who serve as members of the Vestry of the Trinity Episcopal Church in Plattsburgh; Anne-Marie Farrell, who leads study groups at the Plattsburgh Church of the Nazarene and organizes an annual country dance ball for members of the church; and Phyllis Wells, who, as a retired librarian at SUNY Plattsburgh, undertook a history of local churches, including her own parish, the First Presbyterian Church of Plattsburgh.

Peru's Quaker Union also involved the active work of women. In fact, Hulda Hoag held the first Friends Meeting at Peru Union. Along with her husband and four children, Hulda was a recorded minister at the Ferrisburg (Vermont) Quarterly meeting, an acknowledgement that she had the gift of spoken ministry. Other women followed in her footsteps, with Elizabeth Keese Irish, Cynthia Knowles, Mrs. Isaac Hallock and Ruth Hoag all preaching at the Union.

A formal ministry was not required for participation, though. Women also worked to maintain the records of the Quaker Union and to develop an accurate listing of those buried in the Quaker cemetery. Since the early Quakers did not believe in erecting monuments, most of the graves in the burying ground are entirely unmarked or are noted by a piece of fieldstone with a name or initial inscribed. Since those inscriptions have faded over time, the lists, compiled by Pauline Keese and typed during the latter part of the twentieth century by Eleanor Spaulding, constitute an important historic record. Spaulding's interest in the burial ground extended to the organization of the Quaker Union Society in 1950. The group's goals were "to restore the burying ground and improve the site of the first Church in this area, also to bring to the meetings any available facts regarding the early settlers of the community, most of whom were members of the Quaker Church and whose bodies lie buried here." When a historic marker was erected on the site in 1959, Dr. Georgia Harkness attended and spoke at the dedication ceremony.

Local Quaker women were also active in their pursuit of social justice. Caroline Moore, who was married to Noadiah Moore, was noted for her strong antislavery position, refusing even to socialize with a local woman who supported slavery. Similarly, Catharine Keese lamented the hypocrisy of Americans, writing in a June 10, 1830 letter to Sarah Baker, recorded in a posthumous memoir published by her husband and friends, "So, it seems, dear S—, the poor Indians are to be driven off. Do thou *never* boast of being an *American*. Dost thou remember the Greek women's appeal to the ladies

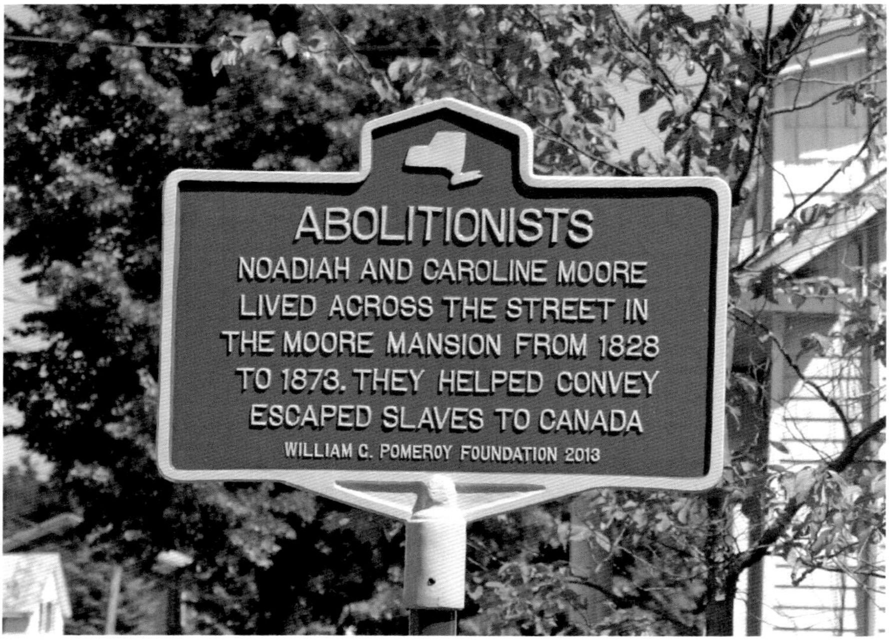

Historic marker dedicated in honor of Noadiah and Caroline Moore, Village of Champlain, 2013. *Author's collection.*

of America? Two of the lines are, 'Daughters of that happy land/Where oppression finds a grave.' It makes me blush to be praised when we do not deserve it. From this period, I fear may be dated the downfall of our country." Her obituary proclaims: "Her heart kept in remembrance the 'sorrowful everywhere,' and none who knew her can forget her dedication to the cause of the oppressed. For many years of her life, she had conscientiously avoided the use of the produce of their labor, and it was her earnest desire that the society in which she ministered might be united in an uncompromising testimony against participation in the sin of Slavery."

Kari Tuling, who has served as the rabbi of Temple Beth Israel, a reform congregation in Plattsburgh since 2012, seeks social justice and equality through her work, as well. In 2013, Tuling—and other members of an organization called the Women of the Wall—went to Israel to challenge the silencing of women that typically occurs within orthodox communities. As she prepared her Erev Yom Kippur sermon, which remembered the fortieth anniversary of the Yom Kippur War, "it became increasingly clear…I needed to be there too. I needed to demonstrate in voice and in presence, that the ultra-orthodox vision of Judaism is just one small slice of a much larger, more colorful, and more inclusive whole."

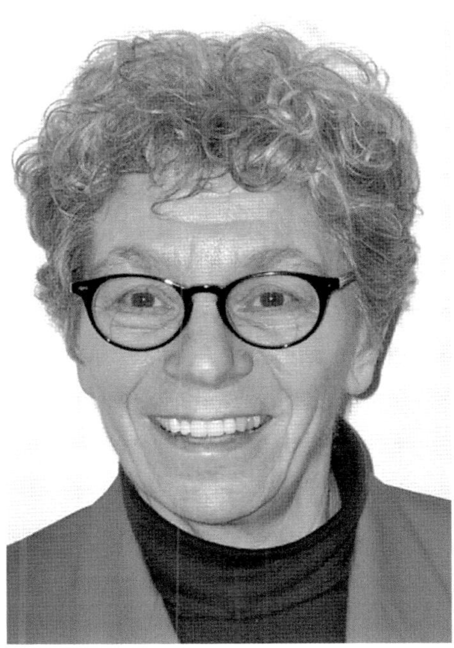

Rabbi Carla Freedman, formerly of the Temple Beth Israel in Plattsburgh. *Clinton County Historian's Office.*

Temple Beth Israel has witnessed several female rabbis, beginning with Carla Freedman, who served from 1990 until 1999. Freedman was the first Canadian woman to be ordained a rabbi at the Hebrew Union College in Cincinnati, Ohio. While in Plattsburgh, Freedman taught courses at Plattsburgh State University. At the beginning of her appointment, she explained in a September 16, 1990 *Press-Republican* article, "For Jewish women traditionally, religious obligations have been optional but not forbidden. Women's traditional focus on the home and child-rearing left little time for the pursuit of scholarly studies... the old sages through childbearing and child-rearing responsibilities would drastically interrupt studies, so women didn't study and they didn't become scholars." The movement into the arena of scholarship and rabbinical study, then, represents a significant movement forward for women. And the people of Plattsburgh were ready for that movement when they hired Freedman. According to members of the search team that hired her, "Members of the Reform movement are accustomed to the idea that a woman can be a rabbi." Heidi Waldmann (2005–2008) and Emma Gottlieb (2010–2012) followed Freedman.

Writing the preface to *From Generation to Generation: The Jewish Congregations of Plattsburgh, N.Y.*, Phyllis Freedman and Susan Ledges explain, "Women have always been the backbone of our Jewish Community. They were the fund raisers and organizers of ritual and social events. With the increasing percentage of women in the work place, the Sisterhood (or Women of Reform Judaism as it is now officially called) is not as active as it formerly was, meeting only a few times a year. However women are still the heart of our congregation, a can-

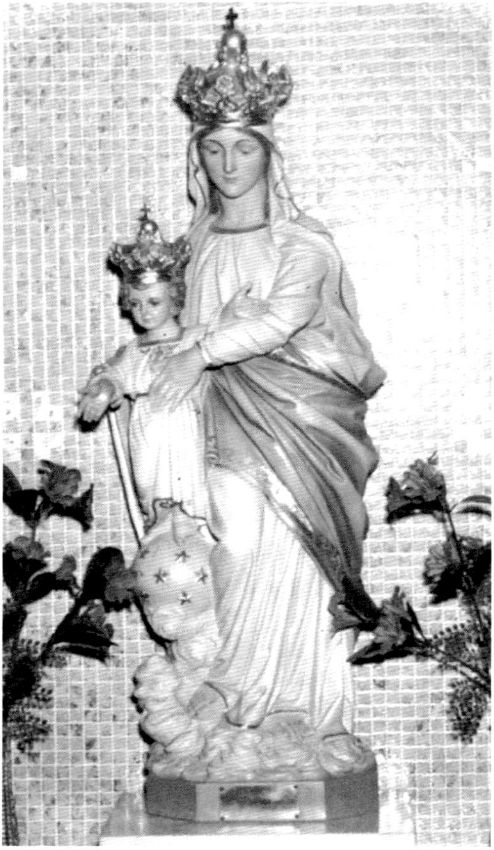

Our Lady of Victory statue. *Clinton County Historian's Office.*

do group providing the weekly Oreg Shabbat, baking the hamentashen, cooking latkes, organizing holiday dinners, etc." Women like Laura Schiff, Beverly Lichtin, Beverly Reuter, Bertha Gordon and Phyllis Freedman have served as presidents of the board, while Beverly Reuter has also served as volunteer cantor since 1985. First organized in 1914, the Beth Israel Sisterhood, with Bertha Gordon serving as the first president, also provides a means for women to gather socially and contribute to "the cultural life of the Temple" and to various other human services agencies in the county.

Religious vocation extends into Clinton County Catholicism, as well. Eleven distinct orders of professed nuns worked within the county beginning in the middle of the nineteenth century, when the Sisters of the Charity of Ottawa came to Plattsburgh. Each order has a distinct mission, though most of them involve education and care of the poor, aged and ill. Encompassing all of northeastern New York, including the Adirondack, Clinton, Essex, Franklin, Hamilton/Herkimer, Jefferson, Lewis and St. Lawrence deaneries, the Diocese of Ogdensburg currently serves a population of 104,113 Catholics; it served a population of 107,648 in 1934 and 129,378 in 1957. Importantly, in 1957, the diocese also included twelve Catholic high schools and thirty-one elementary schools, four Catholic general hospitals, three sanitoria, three schools of nursing, two orphanages and one home for the aged, all of which were served by 584 religious women.

While the work of each of those women was admirable, a few women should be singled out for special attention. The Sisterhood of the Grey

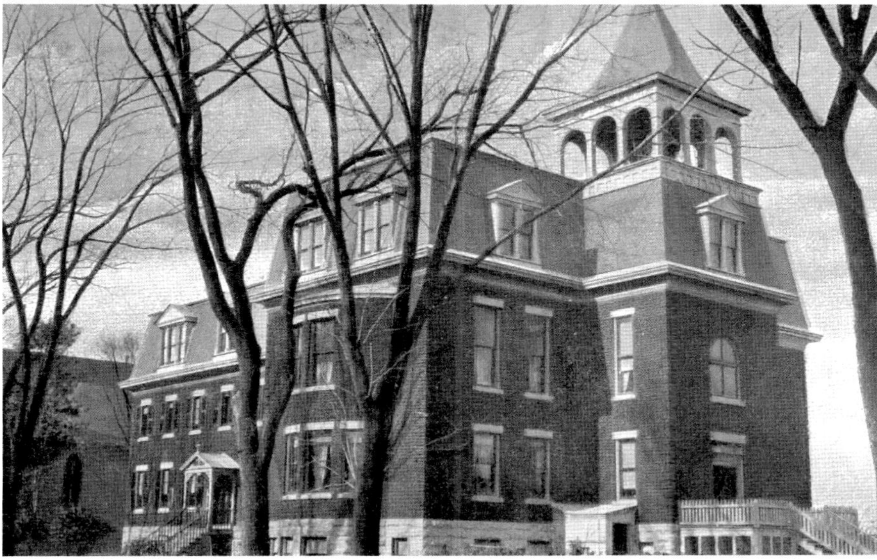

D'Youville Academy, run by the Grey Nuns. *Clinton County Historian's Office.*

Nuns, incorporated on April 6, 1871, played a particularly important role in the history of this region. Devoting themselves to "the education of the young, visiting and alleviating the wants of the poor and sick, and general missionary and benevolent work," the Grey Nuns established D'Youville Academy as a means of fulfilling one of their expressed objectives, "the foundation of an industrial school for girls out of employment." The July 13, 1861 *Plattsburgh Republican* reported D.S. McMasters's praise for the academy and convent:

> *When he referred to the Sisters—their high accomplishments and finished education—their separation from the secular affairs of the world that they might aid fathers and mothers in educating their daughters and fit them to become useful members in society, and act their parts well in society at a future date—how the watchful care of these worthy Sisters, was always present by night and day to protect their pupils and improve their morals, their manners and their information—how that parents might rest assured that their daughters would improve every day in the presence of such teachers, and that this Convent was worthy of public confidence and patronage—he was interrupted with applause from every part of the crowded house.*

With an apostolate focused on education, medicine and social work in the United States and Peru, the Grey Nuns of the Sacred Heart also helped to establish the Champlain Valley Hospital. Concerned with the lack of healthcare in the region, the nuns, led by the Reverend Mother Ann of Jesus, gathered the support of local men like Smith Weed, General Stephen Moffitt and the Honorable J.B. Riley; raised money; and organized the hospital project. The cornerstone for the hospital was laid on July 2, 1906, and the hospital opened on June 22, 1910. While the Grey Nuns and their students at the Champlain Valley Hospital School for Nurses staffed the facility, the hospital was a nonsectarian, general hospital, welcoming patients regardless of their ability to pay or their religious affiliation.

The Congregation of the Sisters of Charity of St. Louis also deserves notice for its work. In 1910, five sisters arrived in Plattsburgh to establish a convent. From that beginning, they created a coeducational high school, a boarding school for girls, a post-secondary secretarial school and a convalescent/nursing home known as the Sacred Heart Nursing Home. Although the schools have all closed, the nursing home, now called Evergreen Valley Nursing Home, continues to serve the region. So do several sisters in the order, including Sister Agnes Racette, a native of Redford who celebrated her Seventy-fifth Jubilee in 2014 and is honored on Seton Catholic Central

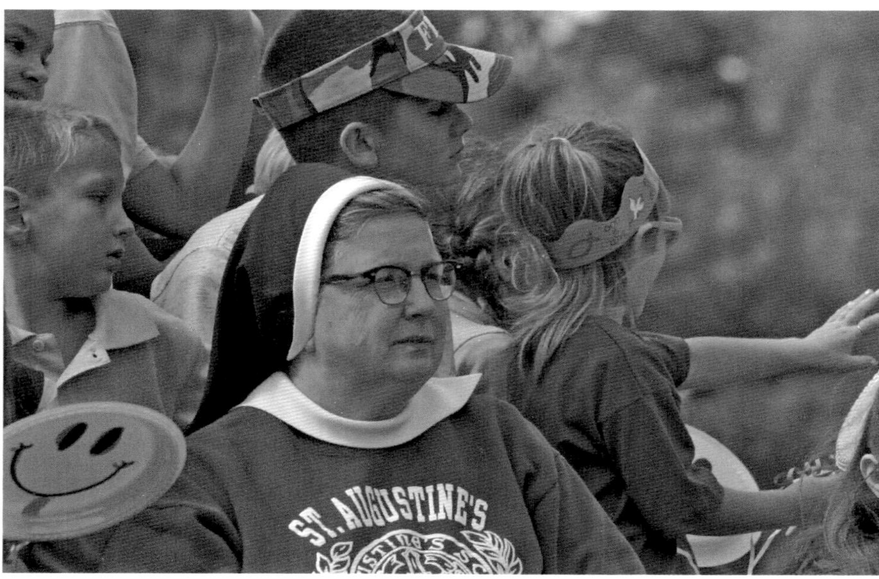

Sister Mary Helen Hermann on a St. Augustine's parade float, circa 2009. *Author's collection.*

School's Clinton County Catholic Schools Wall of Acclaim; Sister Claire Michel Fortier; and Sister Bernadette Ducharme.

Sister Mary Helen Hermann deserves special attention for touching hundreds of lives. As a teacher and principal at St. Augustine's School in Peru and later at Seton Academy, Sister Helen has helped to introduce hundreds of children to the tenets of Catholicism. She has also striven to promote social justice. On December 15, 1995, for example, she wrote a letter to the editor of the *Press-Republican* urging local citizens to take action. "Especially during this holiday season," she wrote, "Americans hope for peace on Earth. The Senate has the opportunity to make the world safer for everyone, despite all the negative events around us, by ratifying the Strategic Arms Reduction Treaty and the Chemical Weapons Convention…As I see it, the U.S. has a once-in-a-lifetime opportunity to take a bold step toward reducing the level of violence worldwide, and to set the course for peace." She urged readers to contact Senate representatives, to act quickly in order to bring about the ratification of the treaties. On February 16, 1996, she urged all media outlets, including the *Press-Republican*, to investigate political action committee funds spent on individual candidates and campaigns. Yet, her political and religious beliefs pale in comparison to her basic humanity. Sister Helen is known by most as a fun-loving jokester who loves to sing and to help kids grow into decent human beings.

For Catholic women, another means of service and religious expression involves joining the Catholic Daughters of the Americas (CDA). Founded in 1903 as "a charitable, benevolent and patriotic sorority for Catholic ladies," the CDA was first called the "National Order of Daughters of Isabella" and was associated with the Knights of Columbus. The organization's principles, "Unity and Charity," guide their actions. During World War I, those actions included serving as nurses and clerical workers, conducting classes in sewing and knitting for the Red Cross and staging parties for servicemen. World War II brought a different type of service: buying war bonds and defense stamps, making bandages, donating blood and conducting first aid classes.

The Catholic Daughters of the Americas have been in Clinton County since the early part of the twentieth century. In Rouses Point, Court Patricia No. 962 was established on May 10, 1925; in Ellenburg, Court Little Rose was founded in the fall of 1938 by fifty women. Court Patricia was honored by the New York State Health Facilities Association in 1998 as Volunteer Organization of the Year for its work at Cedar Hedge Nursing Home. Among the many services performed by the group are weekly rosary prayer sessions

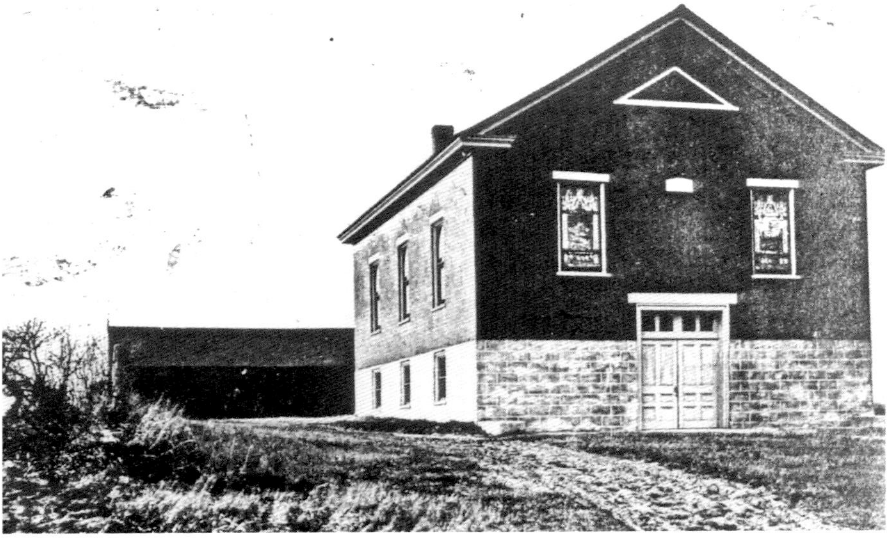

Methodist Episcopal Church, Salmon River community in Plattsburgh. *Clinton County Historian's Office.*

and bingo games, regular visits and special services that, according to Shirley Blair, the quality of life director of the nursing home, go "over and beyond the call of duty with caring and tenderness." Suzanne Moore writes in a June 5, 1998 *Press-Republican* article, "The Catholic Daughters bring varied skills to their ministry. Some knit scarves, mittens and other cozy winter wear or mend residents' clothing. Others just stop in to visit or accompany residents on monthly shopping trips"; they bring home-cooked food to residents and, during the Ice Storm of 1997, did laundry for residents. During its forty-fifth anniversary year, Court Little Rose was featured in a February 24, 1984 *Press-Republican* article, which explained that the group "made donations to the Bishop's Fund, the Knights of Columbus Charitable and Benevolent Program, St. Edmund's Parish fuel collection, the Christmas Bureau, the CCD program at St. Edmund's, altar flowers, the Heart Association, the Cancer Society, Mater Dei College in Ogdensburg, masses for deceased and living members of the court, and local families who have had fires. Also this year, special funds were donated to the Roger Senecal Fund in Plattsburgh and to Father Ritter's Covenant House in New York City. Besides the annual support to the Marie C. Curry Scholarship Memorial Fund, this court also donated to the clergy and the children's and adult's Christmas parties." Court Mary Immaculate 479, in Plattsburgh, was chartered in 1920. Since that time, the group's charitable activities, according to a Feburary 27, 1981 *Press-Republican* article, have been "supported through membership dues, card parties, rummage and book sales and when needed, special projects are undertaken." Among the service offered by Court Mary Immaculate are "many hours of volunteer service at the local nursing homes, the CVPH Medical Center, RSVP, Meals on Wheels, shopping for and visiting shut-ins and working on a one-to-one basis as needs are indicated, plus many more individual acts of goodwill and kindness." CDA courts have been established at many other parishes within the county, as well.

Across the county, a large number of women belong to the CDA. Included among them are Elizabeth Wheeler, Marion Barrett, Rita Farrell, Louise Fallon, Ruth Trudeau, Betty Tousignant, Edith Gwinn, Carleda Taylor, Peg Spiegel, Helen Reynolds, Rita Mischler, Mae Marnes, Frankie Poissant, Wanda Gamache, Lucille Merchant, Florence Bechard, Ila Comeau, Lena Bombardier, Irene Bierer, Ethel Ashline, Helen Boreight, Mary Connelly,

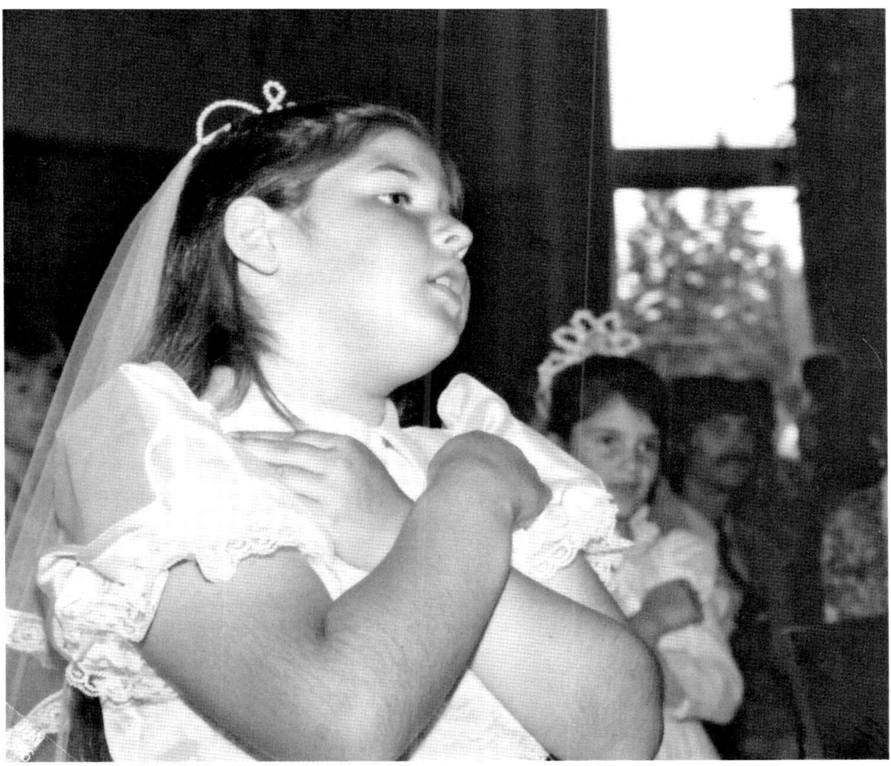

Nicole Pratt Coskey at her first communion, St. Augustine's Church, Peru, 1986. *Author's collection.*

Mary Couture, Grace Couture, Flora Murray, Katherine Moore, Lorena Rivers, Helen Rock, Ida Gooley, Veronica Gratton, Siwa Marnes, Ila Carriere, Flora Murray, Helen Mero, Katie White, Kathryn Deering, Kathryn Daly, Catherine Stanford, Rowena Gardner, Katherine Duffy, Alice Kennedy, Lenora Willette, Eva LeClair, Verda Lashway, Anna Harnett, Anna Bohon, Tina Ashline, Mable LeClair, Minnie Seguin, Christa Covel Reyell, Jean Craig, Lynda Mulcahy, Jane Lafreniere Woods and Julie Ston Liberty.

The Altar Rosary Society offers laywomen another chance to serve the Catholic Church. Although the names of the societies differ, each focuses on caring for its parish's altar and other sacred spaces. The Peru Rosary Society formed in 1939, joining other women's organizations like the Society of the Miraculous Medal. Members care for the altar and chapel at St. Augustine's Church and assist with parish activities; "with the Blessed Virgin as their patron, each member strives to live her life as Mary would have." The society also helps with the Applefest, sponsors a USO dinner and staffs the concessions of the bingo games held by the parish and the Knights of Columbus; members also meet with the Ladies Guild of the Peru Community Church once a year to promote fellowship.

In Chazy, the Sacred Heart Church Altar Rosary Society formed in 1938. The group's parish responsibilities, described by a February 27, 1981 *Press-Republican* article, moved beyond caring for the sacristy and included "training altar boys and supporting CYO activities. They also create unity between parents and church school teachers with special workshops." St. Patrick's Rosary Altar Society, chartered in 1956, offers a slightly different focus, avowing "to say the rosary every day and to care for the church linens and care of the sacristy and altars." The Altar and Rosary Society at St. Edmund's Church in Ellenburg, organized circa 1950, works to "provide whatever may be necessary in the sanctuary."

Every Catholic church in Clinton County includes an Altar Rosary Society. Among the women who have served the church in this capacity are Margaret Spiegel, Josie Langevin, Carolyn Congelton, Agnes Trombley, Nancy Habib, Barbara Matott, Peg Jackson, Madalyn L'Heureux, Marjorie McCarty, Beverly Uliva, Betty Thompson, Pat DeVito, Sarah Clarke, Rose Delumyea, Mary Mussot, Beatrice Jefferson, Phyllis Jefferson, Nellie Duffy, Della Trombley, Irene Trombley, Rose Moore, Bertha Moore, Alice (Peg) Barcomb, Doris Rochester, Ann Honan, Irene Lombard, Helen Wetterby, Eileen Ashline and Theresa Penfield.

Other individual forms of service for Catholic women do exist. Women contribute music to masses, serve as Eucharistic ministers and lectors, teach

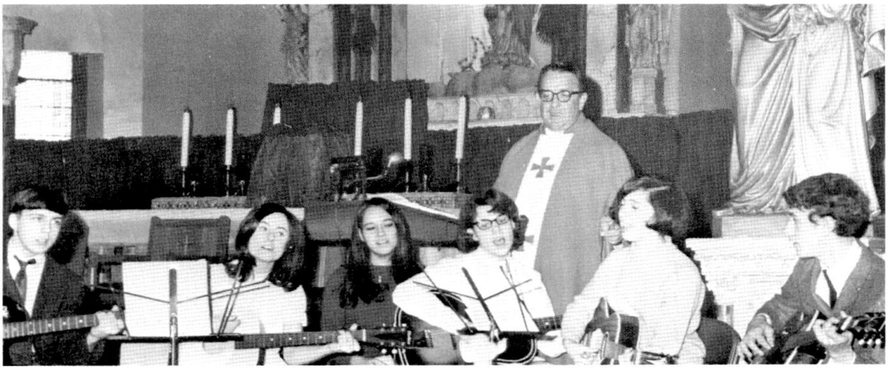

Debbie Payette, Linda Hall, Lori Clukey and Lita Kelly (left to right) perform at a 1968 Folk Mass at OLVA. *Clinton County Historian's Office.*

religious education courses and serve as campus ministers. They work as lay ministers, pastoral associates and administrators. In short, they participate in every facet of Catholic life. Some Clinton County women who warrant special mention for their activities are: Pam Ballantine, who progressed from a volunteer at church to positions as coordinator of the religious education program at St. Alexander's Church, pastoral associate for St. Alexander's and assistant director of education for Catholic Schools and Christian Formation in the Plattsburgh Regional Center for Christian Formation; Jutta Purtell, who, with a group of volunteers, knits, crochets and sews items to give away and to sell as a fundraiser for good works and who also serves as a Eucharistic minister; Mary Hensel, who serves as a lector and, as Eucharistic minister, brings the sacrament of the Eucharist to the sick and homebound; Mary Skillan, who is the director of Campus Ministry at the Roman Catholic Church of St. John the Baptist; Lynn Lynch, who works in her parish office and devotes many hours to religious education and to fundraising activities on behalf of the church; Anne Torrance, who serves as a Eucharistic minister and a member of the St. Augustine's Parish Council; and Maxine Ghrist, who, for years, organized the craft fair for the annual harvest dinner at St. Joseph's Church in West Chazy and continues to work at the dinner, helping to raise money for her parish.

Chapter 6

ARTS AND CULTURE

The cultural life of Clinton County is broad, encompassing a great many historical associations, museums, arts and athletic activities. While the activities undertaken by each of the distinct groups vary greatly, they all underscore a love of this region and an appreciation of the people who live here. Sometimes, as in the case of the annual Mayor's Cup Regatta and the activities to commemorate the Battle of Plattsburgh each year, the many cultural groups of Clinton County come together for parades, dances, races, good food and historical reenactments.

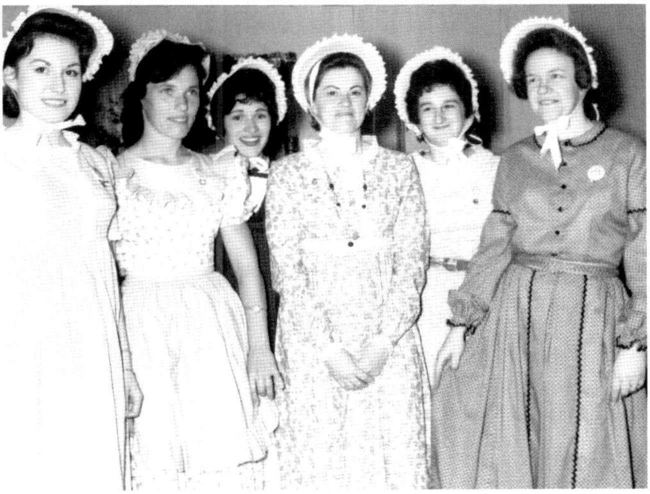

The "Celebration Belles," from the 1964 Battle of Plattsburgh commemoration. *Clinton County Historian's Office.*

HISTORIANS AND HISTORICAL SOCIETIES

One group that takes a particular interest in the region is the Saranac Chapter, Daughters of the American Revolution (DAR). Organized in 1895 with twenty-three charter members, the DAR strives to remember and honor those who died during the American War of Independence. To do that work, members, in 1899, placed bronze markers on the graves of fifteen soldiers buried in Riverside Cemetery. Later, in 1930, they unveiled a flag and plaque at Point au Fer, where Revolutionary War soldiers were buried; in 2009, they rededicated the markers during the 400th anniversary year of Samuel de Champlain's arrival in this region. The group also marks the anniversary of the Battle of Valcour each year, offering a ceremony that remembers the first naval battle of the Revolution, which occurred on Lake Champlain. Membership in the DAR is limited to women who can prove lineal descent from those who fought for American independence during the war, so DAR members often help prospective members trace their family's history back to the Revolution. Local members have included Theodora Kyle, Helen Woodward, Erminia Hall, Leah Drown, Pam Meyers, Amy Sheldrake, Addie Shields, Kate Cleveland Smith, Deborah Gifford, Nancy Smith, Carol Allen and Cynthia Kimmel.

Another historical society in the county, the Clinton County Historical Association (CCHA), offers open membership to anyone interested in local history. Founded in 1945, CCHA "was established to preserve the history of Clinton County, acquire collections and publish county history, in the form of newsletters, pamphlets and books." The group's members started collecting artifacts during their first year, operating at a variety of locations including rooms in the Plattsburgh Public Library and City Hall, at 48 Court Street and in their current building at 98 Ohio Avenue on the former Plattsburgh Air Force Base. CCHA's current mission, "to collect and preserve historical material pertaining to the history of Clinton County and to interpret and celebrate, through exhibits and programs, the County's rich history," places it at the center of local historical pursuits. The group's sponsorship of the McMasters Prize for the Writing of History serves as one way the association encourages the study of local history. Named for Emily Alice McMasters, "a Plattsburgh native and an amateur historian and curator of the Historical Association from 1962 to 1967," who according to an April 5, 1988 *Press-Republican* article, "literally [held] the Historical Association together when we didn't have a home for it," the award started when McMasters's nephew, Daniel, gave his portion of her estate to CCHA

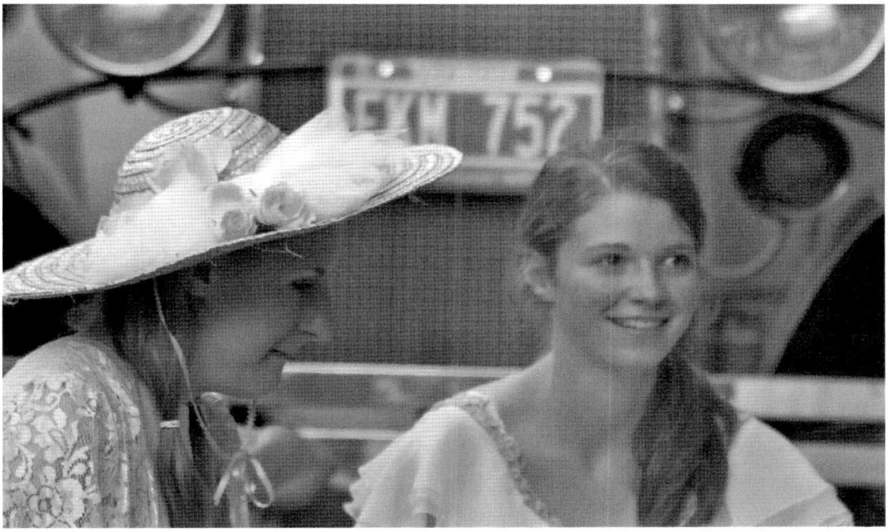

Chazy Central Rural School students, in period costume, participate in the unveiling of a historic marker, 2009. *Author's collection.*

in 1974. Among those who have won the contest are Betty Baldwin (1976), Marjelou Gage (1977), Phyllis Wells (1981), Marcia Moss (1988), Laura Viscome (1997) and Kristina Parker (2003). Curators and directors of the museum have included McMasters, Ruth Hecht, Helen Allan, Jane Rupp, Shirley Koester, Tricia Davies and Melissa Peck. Among those who have worked as docents, board members and volunteers at CCHA are Vickie Morey, Helen Allen Nerska, Julie Dowd, Jan Couture, Mary Nicknish, Heidi Dennis, Geri Favreau, Maurica Gilbert and Judy Estes.

Although CCHA does receive some funding from the Clinton County legislature, it is separate from the office of the Clinton County historian and the offices of other municipal historians throughout the county. Thanks to a 1919 New York State law, every municipality is required to have a historian, someone, Edmund Winslow explains, "in each community who could respond to requests for information on the history of the locality" and "collect and organize local history material and…cooperate with other public officers in the preservation of historically valuable local records." Not surprisingly, many of Clinton County's municipal historians have been women. In fact, the first Clinton County historian was Marjorie Lansing Porter, who is widely remembered as "a pioneer collector of information on the folk traditions of the Adirondacks, an avocation which she pursued alongside her career in journalism until her death in 1973." As Douglas Skopp wrote, "Anything which reflected daily life and popular culture in the Adirondacks was of interest to her. Self-sustained and self-motivated, she made invaluable, although primitive recordings of countless interviews with old-timers, catching songs and stories which otherwise would have been lost. Pete Seeger and others have recorded melodies and lyrics which she recovered, based upon the recordings and notes she made; these are now preserved in the Feinberg Library Special Collections."

Margaret Durkee Hayes also served as Clinton County historian. In a March 18, 1961 *Press-Republican* article, she described her job as the "answering of many inquiries, collecting and preserving historical records" and responding to genealogy requests. Hayes saw her work as one of safeguarding the tenets and values of America. "To preserve our democracy," she said, "we must know how our system emerged in the past. There seems to be no better way than to collect and to preserve the records of the past and the present as guides for posterity." Diana Davis, in 1968, wrote of Margaret, as the Business and Professional Women's "Woman of the Year," "Believing that 'a career is the best thing for a woman,' she has worked most of her life. Her first jobs were in various offices in town and as a court reporter. During World War II, she began working for the Red Cross and stayed with the organization for 16 years. She was selected by the legislature for her current position." Fairly revolutionary for her time, Hayes explained, "After a woman's family has grown and leaves her, a woman must go back to doing the thing she does best. A woman without a career is half alive."

Addie Lawrence Shields was the longest-serving Clinton County historian, beginning her service in 1987 and continuing until 1989 and then serving again from 1996 to 2008. Born in 1916, Addie graduated from the Plattsburgh Normal School (1937), taught in Beekmantown's District 3 from 1937 until 1941 and married Francis Shields in 1940. After her marriage, she had two children and, with her husband, ran the Charles H. Shields Family Farm and Retail Turkey Business. During her long career, Addie served as the chairman of the Women's Committee of the Farm Bureau, the secretary and treasurer of the Northeast Local Dairymen's League, the assistant director of the Migrant Mexican Day Care Center and the town of Beekmantown historian.

Other local historians have taken a similar interest in their hometowns. Mary Fogarty, who served as the town of Plattsburgh historian, spearheaded the town's Bicentennial Committee, producing various programs and an important book, *Historical Sketches of the Town of Plattsburgh, 1785–1975*.

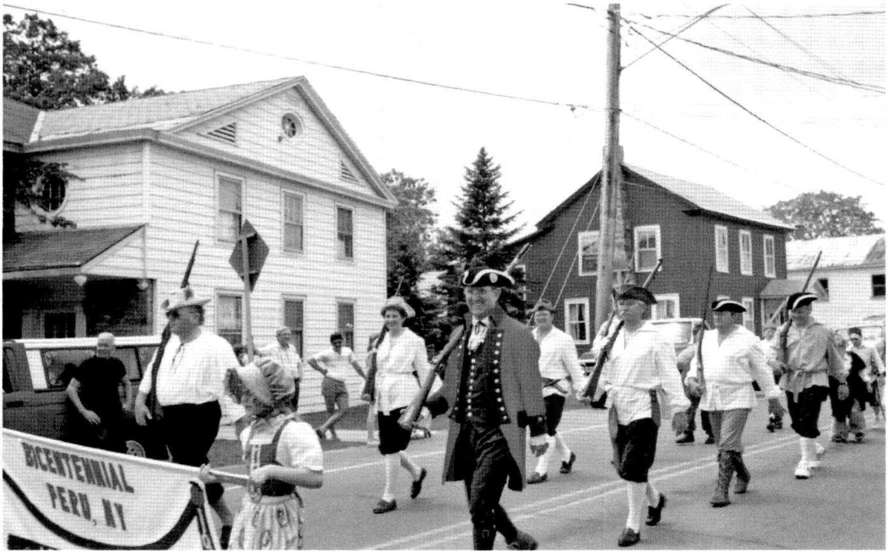

Carol Solari-Ruscoe, a former Social Studies teacher at Peru Central School, joins the Peru Militia, 1992. *Author's collection.*

Lucille Holm, Grace Hagar and several other women worked with Fogarty on that project. Similarly, Beverly Newell, Judy Seymour, Shirley Balko, Betty Brown, Sylvia Burgess, Marion Christon, Myra Decker, Barbara Dorrance, Leona Gadway, JoAnn Hockney, Edda Kelly, Carol McLean and Crystal Russell all served on a committee to recognize the 150th anniversary of the Town of Schuyler Falls in 1998. Currently, Barb Benkwitt and Marge Wood serve the people of Schuyler Falls as historian and deputy historian, respectively.

The town of Chazy has included several dedicated historians, including Nell Barnett Sullivan and Marie Gennett. Born in 1883, Sullivan came to Chazy in 1909, after her marriage to Benjamin Franklin Sullivan. Appointed curator and director of the Alice T. Miner Colonial Home with her husband in the 1940s, Sullivan continued in the position until 1962, adding the position of Chazy historian in 1957. Her passion for history, although present throughout her life, increased greatly after her husband's death, when Sullivan sought ways to occupy her time. In the preface to *A History of the Town of Chazy, Clinton County, New York*, which she wrote with David Kendall Martin, Sullivan's interest is described as such:

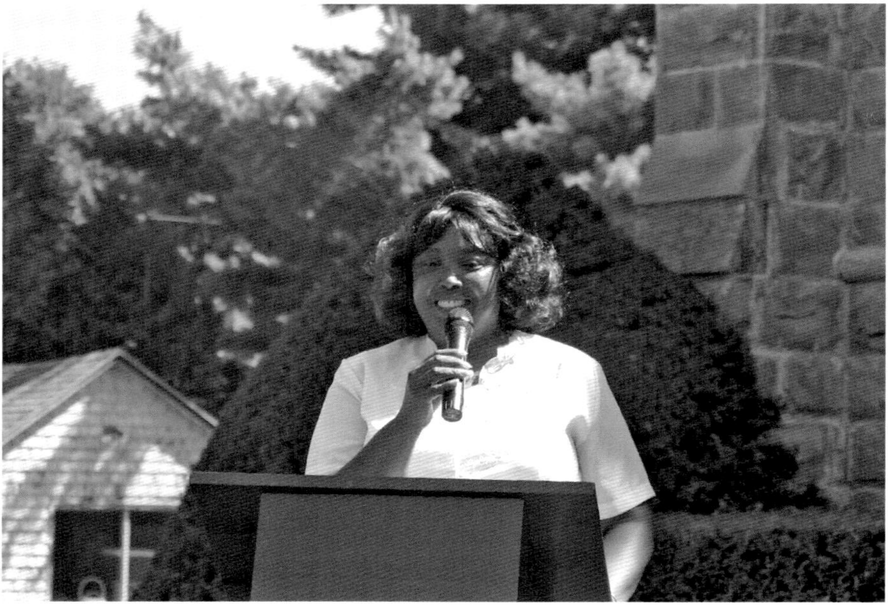

Jackie Madison, president of the North Country Underground Railroad Historical Association, speaks at the unveiling of an historic marker. *Author's collection.*

> *Here was a town over 150 years old, the oldest settled spot in Clinton County, and people were unaware of its background; much of the town's history was already lost, more of it was rapidly disappearing, and no one was doing anything about it! This inspiration led Mrs. Sullivan to abandon her genealogy and undertake to collect, arrange, and preserve what she could of the fragments of town history still available from town and county records, church records, old letters, diaries, newspapers, and the recollections of older people. Her efforts, unsparing in time and expense, have taught her the stories of Chazy and accumulated for the town a magnificent collection of material related to its past. Such service to a community should not go unrecognized.*

Marie Laramie Gennett, "a fifth-generation Chazyite and deputy town clerk," took on the role of historian in 1994, working with her devoted husband, Leon. Although her humor and goodwill set her apart as a woman, Marie's great contribution to the history of Chazy was making the office's collections accessible to researchers. She inherited an impressive number of sources gathered by Sullivan and her daughter, Edith Moss, who took over as historian in the late 1970s but was saddled with an out-of-the-way office at the top of the old Methodist Church building. At Gennett's request, the Historian's Office was given the former Town Clerk's Office and meeting room on the first floor after renovations were completed. Marie Gennett, who described her job as a "labor of love" in a June 20, 1995 *Press-Republican* article, credited Eleanor Martinsen, Joyce LaVoie and volunteers from the Northern New York American-Canadian Genealogical Society for helping to move and organize her office's records, but former town supervisor George Deno reminded the community that "Marie is tireless in her efforts and doing a fantastic job." In 1996, Marie and Leon were honored as the twenty-eighth king and queen of the Chazy Old Home Day by the Chazy Lions Club. Recognized for their "instant recall on past happenings and current events" and described in a July 31, 1996 *Press-Republican* article as "dedicated, determined, concerned matchmates," the Gennetts were active in a wide variety of Chazy events before and after their retirement (Leon from the U.S. Immigration Service and Marie from Wyeth-Ayerst, where she worked in sales and traffic).

The roster of women who served as local, municipal historians is far longer than this, of course. Included among the group are Bridgette Coolidge

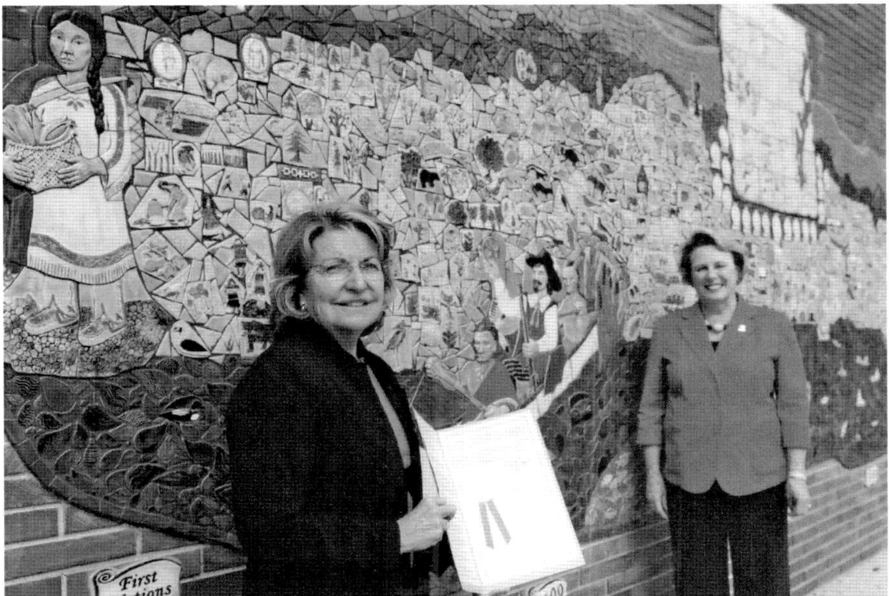

Betty Little (left) and Celine Racine Paquette stand in front of the *Clinton County History Through the Eyes of Its Children* mosaic, 2009. *Clinton County Historian's Office.*

(Altona), Roby Scott (AuSable), Rita Rougeau (Black Brook), Dianne Lagree (Clinton), Ruth LaBombard and Joan Hobbs (Ellenburg), Carol Nedeau and Jennifer Bulriss (Mooers), Carol Allen (Peru), Jan Couture (Saranac) and Peg Barcomb, Donna Racine and Dawn O'Boyle (Rouses Point).

Other historical associations and museums in the area enhance local life. The Alice T. Miner Museum, Anderson Falls Heritage Society, Babbie Rural & Farm Learning Museum, Champlain Valley Transportation Museum, Heart's Delight Farm Heritage Exhibit, Imaginarium Children's Museum, Kent-Delord House Museum, Lyon Mountain Mining and Railroad Museum, North Country Cultural Center for the Arts, North Star Underground Railroad Museum, Northern New York American-Canadian Genealogical Society, Plattsburgh Air Force Base Museum, Plattsburgh State Art Museum, Village of Dannemora Museum and War of 1812 Museum offer invaluable services to the region. Among the women who work with those groups are Gloria Pratt, Barb Benkwitt, Lynn Lynch, Kathy Buckley, Marie Gennett, Eleanor Martinsen, Elizabeth Botten, Barbara Seguin, Julie Dowd, Pam Meyers, Fran Lemery, Patricia Loughan, Anne Bailey, Sharon Bell, Joyce Rafferty, Donna Bell, Sally Booth, Scarlett McBride, Carol Lindberg, Deanne Price, Joanne Astill, Jessica Spiegel, Susan Hale, Monica McGaughey, Karen Dispo-DeBoos, Connie Miller, Karen Bouvier, Ellen Adams, Jacqueline Madison, Linda Richardson, Sue Crowningshield, Kathleen LaVoie, Helen Nerska and Bev Papson.

During the celebration of the Hudson-Fulton-Champlain Quadricentennial in New York State, students from across Clinton County, working with their teachers and local historians, created a thirty-eight-foot-long ceramic tile mosaic called *Clinton County History Through the Eyes of Its Children*. Proposed by Sandra Morse, a retired teacher, the mosaic shows moments from the county's past, beginning before European settlement and continuing through the end of the nineteenth century. With Morse, artists Sue Burdick Young and Bucky Seiden oversaw the design and creation of tiles, while Clinton County historian Anastasia Pratt developed the timeline and helped fourth- and seventh-grade students from every school in Clinton County research people and events significant to their portion of the timeline. Beyond its ability to present local history in an appealing visual manner, the mosaic bridges the gap between history and the fine arts, which have a long and vibrant history in the region.

VISUAL, PRINT AND FOLK ARTS

One example of the fine arts at work in Clinton County is Nina Winkel. Born in Germany in 1905, Winkel and her husband immigrated to the United States in 1942, fleeing the Nazi regime. Settling in New York City, where she became the first woman in the city to acquire a welding certificate and, in 1945, became a naturalized citizen, Winkel continued to pursue her art. In 1954, the Winkels moved to Keene Valley, in Essex County. During her career, Nina's art was greatly praised. Honors included an exhibition at the Metropolitan Museum of Art in 1951, the Samuel F.B. Morse Medal in 1964, the E. Watrous Gold Medal in 1964, the bronze medal in the National Sculpture Society in 1967, an honorary doctorate of fine arts from Plattsburgh State University and inclusion in both *Who's Who of American Women* and *Who's Whom in the World.*

Nina Winkel's connection to Clinton County started in 1983, when she chose PSU as the repository for her works. Along with the donation of sculptures, drawings and sculpture studies, the Winkels funded a sculpture court to house the works of art. Dedicated on October 24, 1987, the Nina Winkel Sculpture Court is an enclosed atrium on the second floor of the Myers Fine Arts Building. Pat Crosby, a rare woman in the field of construction, built the gallery, which is "one of the largest spaces in the country devoted to art created by a woman." Edward Brohel, former curator and director of the collection, explained that the Winkels' bequest "is a comprehensive view of fifty years of her creative

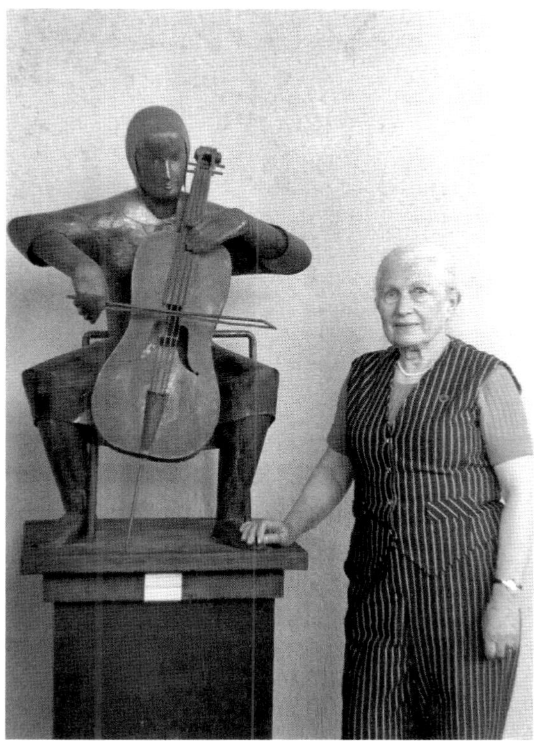

Nina Winkel stands next to her sculpture *Brahms Concerto* (1963). *The Plattsburgh State Art Museum.*

accomplishments. A philosophy of life animates the sculpture, while its formal and historical references include 20th century German expressionist art and late medieval religious and folk art of southern Germany. Opposing this expressionist direction, a strong current of classical interest is present, both in the iconography and the full balanced contours of the form."

In their final will and testament, George and Nina Winkel further endowed the Winkel Bequest and Trust Fund of the Plattsburgh College Foundation. Besides continuing to fund the Winkel Sculpture Court and the Nina Winkel Sculpture Collection and Archives, the bequest generates money for the Plattsburgh State University Art Museum and provides special funds for student scholarships and faculty development in the Visual Arts and Humanities. A huge number of working artists have emerged from that art department over the years.

Local artists, some associated with PSU and others not, work and show their art in Clinton County. Some of the most famous among them are Jackie Sabourin, a potter and retired art teacher, for whom the North Country Cultural Center for the Arts has named its clay studio; Lynn Manning, another retired art teacher whose art combines photography and mixed-media art; Tory Taber, an adjunct professor at PSU who produces collaborative illustrations with her husband, Norman; Carol Hochreither, an artist whose works include watercolors, collages, pastels, oils and acrylics; Diane Fine, a professor of art at PSU and a printmaker; Judy Guglielmo, a painter and real-estate agent; and Della White, the great-granddaughter of Jacques Rouse, who painted in her Rouses Point studio for several years.

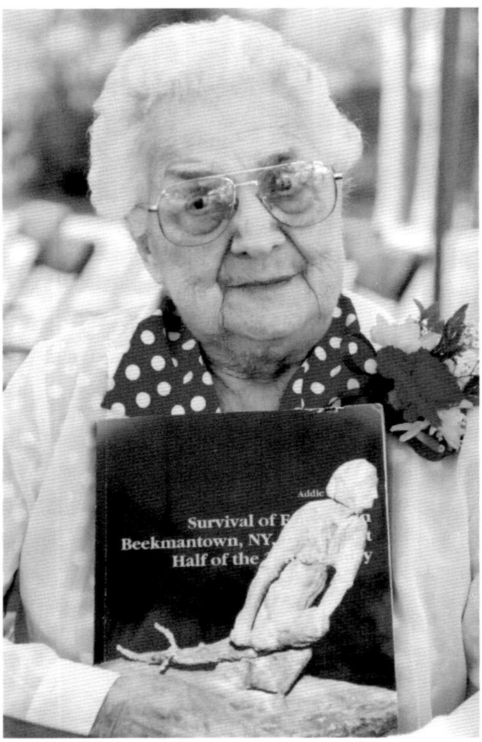

Addie Lawrence Shields, with her memoir, at a history festival, 2009. *Clinton County Historian's Office.*

Beyond the fine arts, local residents have been active as folk artists. Textiles were particularly popular as a medium, especially since women have long been taught needlework as a practical skill. Sophia Moore, daughter of Pliny and Martha, and her adopted sister Harriet Hicks were noted for the cross-stitch needlework floor coverings they created. Possibly the "oldest surviving needlework floor coverings in the country," according to Allan Everest, "All of the materials for the project were produced on the farm except the canvas backing, which was procured in Montreal. The larger piece is now a prized object in the Americana Wing of the Metropolitan Museum in New York City; it was completed on March 1, 1811. The smaller one, with its hunting design, is equally treasured by the Museum of the Clinton County Historical Association in Plattsburgh."

Other local women have crocheted, knitted, embroidered and sewed treasured objects. Among them are Pauline White, Yvonne Comeau, Elizabeth Fitts, Elfriede Mozzicato, Thelma Pinsonnault, Gladys Pray, Dorothy Bodette, Celina Spoor, Constance McNally, Frances Hadcock and Donna Trombley. Those who have focused on quilting, displaying their works for historical celebrations and artistic showings, include Judith Bunnell, Linda LaMarche Harwood, Jean Welch, Barb Stadnicki, Victoria Evans, Mary Gagne Durocher and Gladys Stiles.

Local women have also been active as writers. Lucretia and Margaret Davidson were widely known for their poetry. After Lucretia's early death, her mother published a book of her poems, which included "Reflections, On Crossing Lake Champlain in the Steam-Boat Phoenix":

Islet on the lake's calm bosom,
In thy breast rich treasures lie;
Heroes! there your bones shall moulder,
But your fame shall never die.
Islet on the lake's calm bosom,
Sleep serenely in thy bed;
Brightest gem our waves can boast,
Guardian angel of the dead!
Calm upon the waves recline,
Till great Nature's reign is o'er;
Until old and swift winged time
Sinks, and order is no more.
Then they guardianship shall ceased,
Then shall rock they aged bed;
And when Heaven's last trump shall sound,
Thou shalt yield thy noble dead!

Other writers whose works celebrate this region include Grace W. Wilson, Myra Magoon White and Addie L. Shields. Wilson's poem about Peru waxes nostalgic for an earlier time: "Peru, a name that so often means / A country large and far away / But to me, my home that's vastly changed / So much more than I can say / If some old timer should return / And gaze with eyes now dim, / He'd never know the old home town / That was home for him… Oh! Those were quiet peaceful days / When only horses roads would plod. / I wonder what is coming next. / The answer lies with God." White's history of Ellenburg was undertaken throughout her life. John W. Harrold describes her undertaking, writing, "As a housewife, she cared for her family and participated in the community activities. Also, it appears she had an interest in and aptitude for local history. It is not known when or how long she collected local lore, but it is known that she wrote over 150 pages about the history of Ellenburg on the back of Ford Motor Company business forms." Finally, Addie L. Shields wrote *Survival of Families in Beekmantown, NY, in the First Half of the 20th Century*, preserving the stories of her beloved home town.

They have been joined by various other female writers, including: Kelly Julian Sexton, Christina Recore, Kimberly Lamay and Celine Racine Paquette, all of whom have written books in Arcadia Publishing's Images of America series; Kathy L. Baumgarten, who wrote *Strictly a Loner: My Life and Times with Plattsburgh's Poorest Millionaire* and *An Away Manger: Twelve Christmas Stories*; Kate Messner, who has written several novels, chapter books, picture books and historical novels centered on Lake Champlain and a book for educators; and newspaper reporters like Keshia Clukey, Robin Caudell, Lois Clermont, LaVerne Dutcher, Suzanne Moore and Susan Tobias.

Many of the works of local writers have been made available to the public through the efforts of women concerned with establishing libraries and literary societies. The Keeseville Public Library, for example, published *Old Keeseville Tales* after the Ladies Library Association staged a series of local history programs in 1900, during which, as Virginia Westbrook explains, "people shared their recollections of early days in the village. So many people wrote to say they wished to be there, or sent their contributions so late, that the library association published the correspondence." That collection included Mrs. Colles's description of the Keese House; Phoebe Macomber Searle's account of the AuSable Chasm, which was not a celebrated landmark during the early part of the nineteenth century; and Emma Learned Kingsland's story of Anna Woodman.

In Peru, the library was created through the efforts of a community group that first met on June 28, 1915, to discuss the need for a library. Within two years, the Peru Free Library had been established, with Edith Stafford as the librarian. Serving in a facility with 943 books, Stafford collected city newspapers beginning in December 1917 and sent them to Peru boys completing military service. During the 1920s, one local woman offered a children's story hour every Tuesday. When Stafford died in 1925, the trustees staffed the library until March of that year, when Mrs. Patrick Fitzpatrick was appointed librarian and Miss Anne Bentley was appointed assistant librarian. When Mrs. Fitzpatrick resigned in 1966, Mildred Bromley was appointed to fill the vacancy. Then, in 1967, Jane Metcalfe took the position. Mary Kay Rillahan and Becky Pace have followed as directors of the library.

Local Friends of the Library groups have provided support for all of the libraries within the Clinton-Essex-Franklin Library System. Included among the women who have made those groups, whether informally or formally organized, are Rose Arno, Joyce LaBombard, Alban Chilten, Elaine Rowe, Florence Gibson, Eloise McGregor, Mary Jane Chilton, Pat Loughan, Kim Bailey, Alix Heuston, Kathy Murnane, Helen Ianelli, Linda

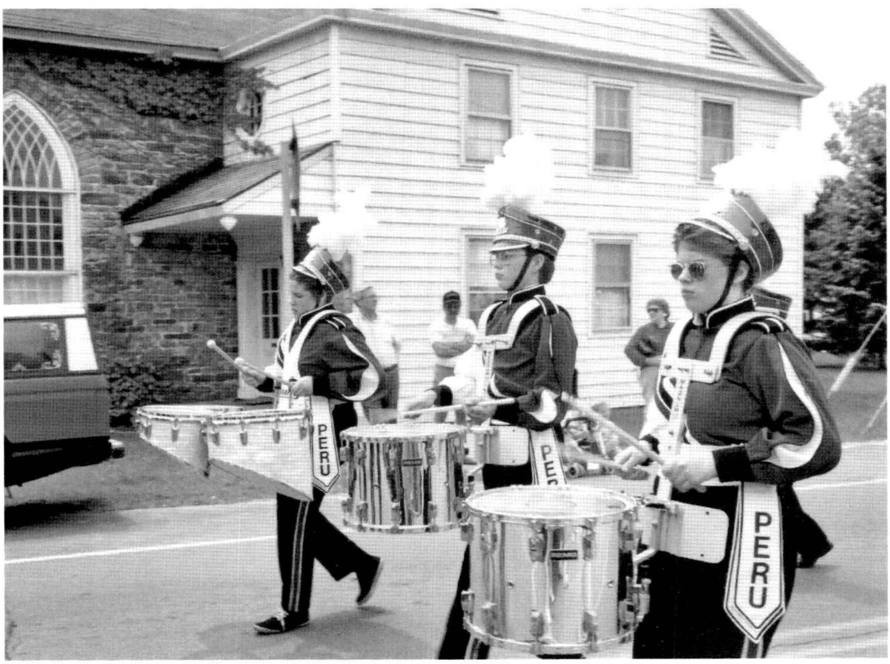

Nicole Pratt Coskey (left) and Jennifer Jenkins (right) keep the beat for the Peru Central School marching band, 1992. *Author's collection.*

Parks, Bobbie Scales, Dotte Buchanan, Rachel Patterson, Elsa Sorley, Joan Dermatis, Doreen Meyer, Eileen Perras, Louise Tanner, Keitha Farney, Sally McSweeney, Jean Tolosky, Kathy Herlihy, Judy Rose, Elsie Waterman and Judy Gallinger.

The Performing Arts

Occasionally, local libraries have served as venues for dramatic performances, particularly in the form of dramatic readings. However, other theater groups have made their home in Clinton County. Beyond the local schools, most of which sponsor an annual musical, if not a full array of dramatic performances, the Chazy Music Theatre serves as an important venue for dramatic performances in Clinton County. The group, which started in 1989, offers an annual musical in which local residents perform on stage and assist with every part of the production, from costumes to properties, makeup, lighting, technical crew, set design and construction, tickets and ticket sales, program design, publicity, orchestra and chaperones for rehearsals and performances. Among the women who have been involved in their productions are Sue Sweet, Cara Congleton, Angie Bouchard, Jess Fairchild, Monique Bedard, Tania Parrott, Mary Kate Gardner, Sara Munson, Maeghan McDonald, Rebecca Boire-West, Sandra Stortz, Tiana Marrero, Suzanne Fountain Deyo, Manda May, Bridget Murphy, Amanda Finckel, Carlinda Mahoney, Rebecca Shuman, Jolee Yeddo, Mio Ottinger, Anastasia Pratt, Celia Strebendt, Kate Bullock, Carolyn Wilson, Susan Nystoriak, Deborah Zink, Sandee Runnells, Jackie Robertin, Kathy Donnelly-Kokes, Hillary Soulia, Kim Howley, Sonia Shivokevich, Rini Green, Bonnie Black and Lydia West.

Musical and dramatic performances in the region began in the nineteenth century. Saranac's Academy Hall, for example, hosted a March 11, 1882 concert in which several women performed. Anna Morhous played the organ for the show, sang twice with a vocal quartet that included Martha Ayres and two professors and performed a vocal solo. Etta Flanders and Maria Davis graced the stage with a dramatic performance the same day. Later musicians in the region included Joanne Coffey Wilke, who taught music at the elementary school in Peru, accompanied countless soloists and school musicals and played piano for St. Augustine's Church, as well. Michelle Davis, a violinist from Plattsburgh, proceeded to study at the Cleveland Institute of Music's Young Artists Program and the University of Michigan, where she earned a bachelor's of music, a masters of violin

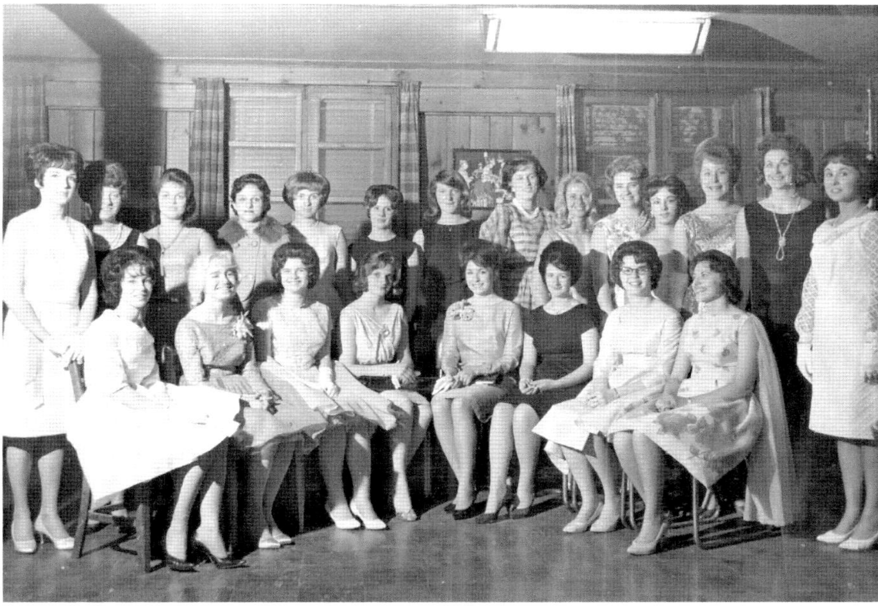

Women participating in a 1964 beauty pageant as part of the Battle of Plattsburgh 150th anniversary commemoration. *Clinton County Historian's Office.*

performance and a masters of chamber music. While a student in the city, Davis performed with the Adirondack Youth Orchestra; she now plays with the Colorado Springs Philharmonic and the Colorado Ballet Orchestra, while maintaining a violin studio, as well.

Carol Davis Gallagher is another local musician of note. A native of Peru, Gallagher studied music at Boston University and teaching at the University of Vermont. She taught music at Peru Central School and served as choir director at the Peru Community Church. Although Carol is, principally, a pianist, her musical skills are far greater than that. Over the years, she has become quite skilled on clarinet, double bass, trombone and trumpet, to name just a few of the instruments she plays. Gallagher is an excellent vocalist and choir conductor as well.

Beyond church choirs, local vocalists have established several groups with which to perform. Chief among these are Champlain Valley Voices, once known as the Champlain Valley Oratorio Society, and the Champlain Valley Sweet Adelines, which began on December 9, 1968. According to Diane Sabourin, the musical style of the group is barbershop, "a cappella music characterized by its tight four-part harmonies and ringing overtones and is

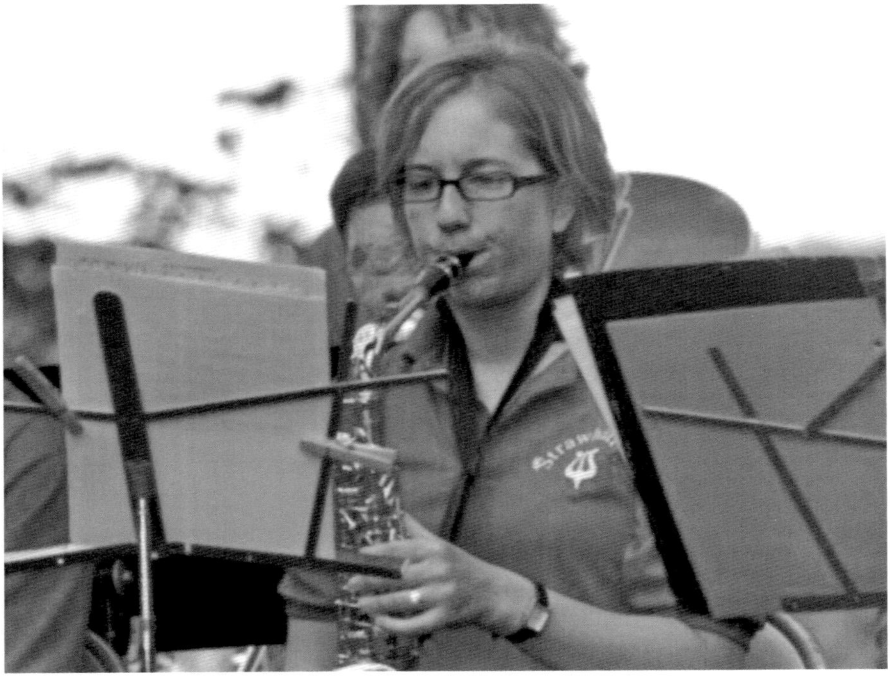

Rebecca Shuman plays with the Strawhatters at the dedication of a historic marker in Chazy, 2009. *Author's collection.*

one of the few exclusively American vocal styles. Although originally sung by men, barbershop singing came to light for women in 1945, when barbershop wives were invited to meet and sing. Its purpose and goal was educational, to teach and train its members in musical harmony and appreciation." From its beginnings, the Champlain Valley chorus has included, at times, up to five quartets and has sponsored six-week summer SINGsation workshops to introduce women to the art of barbershop singing. The group has also sponsored barbershop workshops for teenagers. Included among the women who have performed with the Sweet Adelines are Cherie LaDuke, Diane Sabourin, Carole Harsh, Carla Brassard, Jennifer Scofield and Phil Bernard.

Champlain Valley Voices (CVV), which began in 1983, involves an entirely different choral experience. Rather than barbershop and quartet music, CVV is "dedicated to promoting choral music of the highest artistic quality to stimulate a greater community understanding, appreciation, and enjoyment of choral music." The group's mission is "to provide audiences and singers with a fun and inclusive experience, involving popular literature in a more casual performance environment, as well as orchestral music at the highest level." Among the works performed over the years are oratorios by Handel and Mendelssohn, cantatas by Bach, masses by Hayden and Mozart, and masterworks of various twentieth-century composers. Women who have performed with the chorus include: Pamela Tetreault; Angela Brown; Barbara West; Carol Carpenter (piano); Janice Tobin; Cathie Davenport; Jo Ellen Miano; Suzanne Van Arragon; Wendy DeMane; Barbara Benkwitt; and Helen Anders Kho.

Kho, along with many local music teachers, also helped to create the Adirondack Youth Orchestra Association (AYOA) in order to provide musical opportunities for their students. Beginning in 1985, the group was created when teachers and parents lamented the lack of orchestral possibilities within the county. (Although every school district has a music program that includes a chorus and band, only Peru Central School and the Plattsburgh City School District continue to have orchestral and string programs.) Elizabeth Gorevic, a concert violinist and teacher, was one of the group's organizers; she also helped to develop the string training orchestra in 1993, which later evolved into the Adirondack Youth Strings, Adirondack Youth Mezzo and Adirondack Youth Winds. These beginning groups help to introduce students to orchestral music and performance, preparing them for eventual membership in the Adirondack Youth Orchestra. In 2013, AYOA added two choral groups, Adirondack Youth Voices and Adirondack Youth Choir. Over the years, AYOA has featured several female conductors, including Elizabeth Stoyanovich, Kate Bulluck, Casey Ann Dean Fitzsimmons, Corinne Bennett, Cherie LaDuke and Megan Yonteff.

Other local musicians have included Edith Stafford; Agnes Morgan Hallock; Carrie Hallock; Ida Sharron; Julie Burdo; Cora Macomber Stafford; Nancy Barber; Carol Bradley; Carolyn Marks; Debbie Menzel; Barbara Jarvis; Christine Tessier; Nancy Johnson; Susan Onofrio; Nancy Johnson; Linda McNicholas; Karla Barror; Debbie Jones; Joanne Eccles; Myra Watson; Blanche Smith; Kate Honsinger; Ida Plumley; Gertie Lasalle; Linda Sullivan; Karin Ryan; Julie Venne Hogan, of the local bluegrass and country band Bear Tracks; Jeanettte Woodruff; Rebecca Shuman; Penny Wiese; Lois Allenson; Camelia Ann Provost; Lorraine Smith, Corliss Peterson and Josephine Spear with the Kitchen Band; Mina Sherman, of the Happy Ramblers; Laura Kane Allen; and Dorian Bunting.

Dance, which combines the artistic and the athletic, has been popular in the area since the nineteenth century, when Mrs. Deshons opened her dance school. Others who have taught and studied dance, choreographed

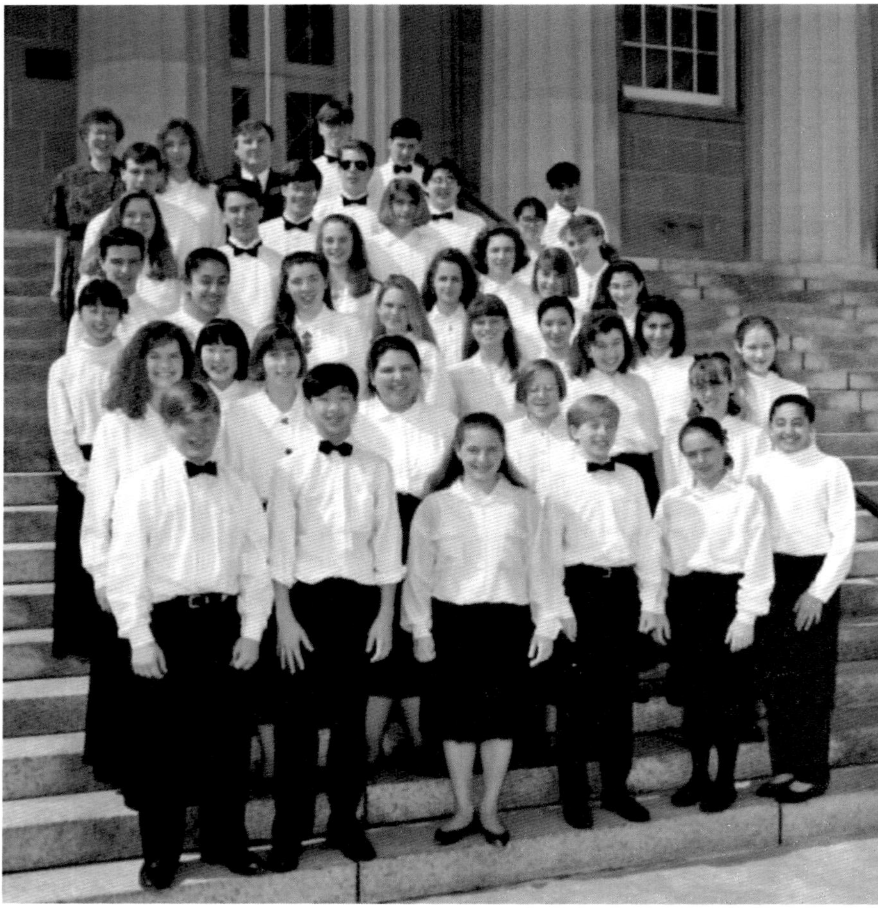

The Adirondack Youth Orchestra on the steps of City Hall, circa 1993, with Helen Kho (upper left) and Michelle Davis (front center). *Author's collection.*

local shows and participated in square dancing include Jackie Robertin, Hilda Lafontaine, Evelyn Erving, Theresa Brenza, Laura Knew Lemon, Josephine Rudmin, Nanc Van Leeuwen, Patricia Langlois Racine, Mercydes O'Connor, Carole Seymour, Evelyn Garrant Donahue, Ruth Hughes, Janine Kemp, Nancy Langlois Gerace, Susan Gerace Mossey, Piper Bruce, Heather Van Arsdel, Amanda Plessis-Belair, Antonette Knodl, Mallory Walk, Kym Taylor, Bonnie Black, Marne Timon, Kelsey Guibord-Stay, Danielle Girard and Deborah Guibord-Stay.

Athletics

Women have also been actively involved in athletic endeavors throughout the region. From the Plattsburgh State Cardinals Women's Hockey Team, which has won three NCAA national titles and has sent several women to the NCAA All-Tournament Team, to the women who regularly run races and complete marathons, Clinton County has a lot of standout athletes. Included among their ranks are Sara Facteau, who ran track and cross country at Peru Central School in the early 1990s and has continued to run since graduation. In 2011, Sara won the Mohawk Hudson River Marathon at the Corning Preserve in Albany, one of the perhaps hundreds of races in which she has run.

Organized fitness programs have brought countless local women to athletic pursuits. CrossFit has become increasingly popular in the area as well, with women like Willow Nolland and Mary Swanson participating in the training, which includes weightlifting, gymnastics and high intensity cardio conditioning and drills. Zumba classes, which use elements of aerobic workouts and dances ranging from hip-hop to salsa, samba to merengue and mambo, are similarly popular. Women like Rebecca Boire-West, Tracy Posada and Lori Walker lead classes throughout the county.

Other standout athletes from the region include Laurie Wood, who grew up in Peru and is now a member of the U.S. Paralympics women's ice sledge hockey team; Donna Dixon, who was inducted into the Cardinals Sports Hall of Fame in 2004 in recognition of her role as a member of the Plattsburgh State Women's Basketball team and who won the Mountain Valley Athletic Conference "Coach of the Year" award in 2012, after seventeen years of service as coach to the conference-winning Clinton Community College Women's Basketball team; Melissa Lahtinen-Penfield, who returned to Plattsburgh High School to coach the Girls Varsity Swim Team from 1992 until 1996 and for whom a city park is named; and Mary Latremore, who was a supporter of all Chazy School athletics and in whose honor the Mary Latremore Memorial "Be the Match" Tournament is sponsored by the girls hockey team.

CONCLUSION

The many remarkable women who helped to create Clinton County deserve to be recognized for their efforts. Whether their stories are already captured elsewhere, as is the case for Katherine Bartoszek, registered on the American Immigrant Wall of Honor at Ellis Island or remembered locally for their good works, as with Elizabeth Sailly Warren, who founded the local League for Control and Protection of Animals, we must share their histories. We need to value the lives of women like Ruth Marnes Edgerton, whose family said that she "will be remembered as a kind and loving person, one who placed everyone's needs before her own" and explained that "her legacy includes the making and giving of many blueberry pies, jams, jellies and chili sauce." Similarly, we must recall the legacy of women like Dr. Ruth Foljambe Copeland who graduated from the University of Rochester Medical School in 1931 and took over as the school and town doctor for Peru in 1943, when Dr. Weeks was called to serve in World War II. After Weeks returned from service, Copeland studied to become an anesthesiologist at the Champlain Valley and Physicians Hospitals, remaining in the profession until she turned seventy.

We must also notice that women's lives involve many different activities. Rarely, if ever, does a woman focus on one job or belief or endeavor. Indeed, women's lives involve a whole host of occupations, ranging from their family lives to their work, from their studies—however formal—to their service to the community, from their faith to their interest in arts and culture. In honoring the women of the past and the women of the present, we must notice those varied pursuits. For the historic record to be accurate, we must recognize that women like Margaret Wilson were loving wives, mothers and friends but also professionals. Indeed, Wilson, who was from Keesville, illustrated *Dick and Jane* readers and workbooks. In calling attention to the most famous of local citizens, like the actress Jean Arthur, who was born in Plattsburgh, we must not forget women like Cosette Aspinall, a registered nurse whose son died during the Vietnam conflict, making her a Gold Star Mother; Lillian Roach, a farm wife who graduated from the Potsdam Normal School and was actively involved in parish life at St. John's Church and in service to the larger community; or Bertha Lowi, who spent two and a half years in a concentration camp during World War II, becoming a U.S. citizen in October 1946.

Their stories are our stories.

BIBLIOGRAPHY

Abell, Susan. "Dogpatch Stage Is Set in Chazy." *Press-Republican*, March 2, 1990, 8.

"About Behavioral Health Services North." http://www.bhsn.org/about.php (accessed October 8, 2014).

"About the Diocese." http://www.dioogdensburg.org/about.html (accessed October 18, 2014).

"About NYSUT." http://www.nysut.org/about/ (accessed October 20, 2014).

"About Order of the Eastern Star." http://www.easternstar.org/information/about-order-of-the-eastern-star/ (accessed October 4, 2014).

"About Us—About Girl Scouts of Northeastern New York." http://gsneny.org/about-us/ (accessed October 5, 2014).

"Act of October 28, 1919 [Volstead Act], 10/28/1919." http://research.archives.gov/description/299827. (accessed October 16, 2014).

"Adirondack Youth Orchestra Association." http://www.ayoa.org/index.html (accessed October 19, 2014).

"American Gold Star Mothers, Inc." http://www.goldstarmoms.com/WhoWeAre/History/History.htm (accessed October 4, 2014).

Baker, Sarah. *The Saranac Valley*. Three volumes. Plattsburgh, NY: Central Printing, Clinton County Government Center, 1985.

Barcomb, Peg. *Rouses Point: 1877 Centennial Year 1977*. Rouses Point: n.p., 1977.

Bartoszek, Monica. "Youth Orchestra Plans 2 Concerts for 1st Year." *Press-Republican*, September 7, 1985, 8.

"Beaumont Papers," archival collection, Department of the Army, the U.S. Army Military Institute, Carlisle, PA.

Bell, Bevera Loudon. "Get Involved in Girl Scouting." *Press-Republican*, December 18, 1993, 4.

"Books." http://www.katemessner.com/books/ (accessed October 19, 2014).

Booth, Alan. Written correspondence with Jim Bailey, 1998.

Brohel, Edward R. "Nina Winkel, Clay Drawings." http://organizations.plattsburgh.edu/museum/ninawinkel.htm (accessed October 7, 2014).

Burdick, Virginia Mason. *Love & Duty: Letters & Diaries of the Delord-Webb Women, 1794–1913*. Plattsburgh, NY: Wiki Publications, 1987.

The Burgh. Various issues.

Cardinal Points. Various issues.

Caudell, Robin. "Bits of Home Sweet Home in Plattsburgh Quilt Exhibit." *Press-Republican*, September 11, 2014, http://www.pressrepublican.com/news/article_0e88e3a0-9ec9-52d5-a257-6116458d4380.html.

———. "City Hall, Library Previously Housed Museum Collection." *Press-Republican*, October 18, 1992, 24.

———. "Community Ready for First Woman Rabbi." *Press-Republican*, September 16, 1990, 25.

———. "Dental Pioneer Honored." *Press-Republican*, March 28, 1999, A4.

———. "Despite Closing, No Sorrow for Sister Theresa." *Press-Republican*, May 31, 1993, 3.

———. "Local Group Looking for Writing worthy of the McMasters Prize." *Press-Republican*, November 9, 1998, 6.

———. "New Rabbi Non-Traditional in Many Respects." *Press-Republican*, September 16, 1990, 25 and 34.

———. "Plattsburgh Nun Celebrates Dodranscentennial." *Press-Republican*, October 24, 2014, http://www.pressrepublican.com/news/plattsburgh-nun-celebrates-dodranscentennial/article_b91ebb79-0ffb-5a9e-8831-fc01ec4c2e4f.html.

"CDA History." http://www.catholicdaughters.org/history.shtml. (accessed October 18, 2014).

"Champlain Valley Educational Services." http://www.cves.org/cv-tec/cv-tec.shtml (accessed October 18, 2014).

"Champlain Valley Voices." http://www.champlainvalleyvoices.org/ (accessed October 16, 2014).

"Chazy Graduates Plan to Continue Their Studies." *Plattsburgh Press-Republican*, September 6, 1957, 2.

"Chazy Music Theatre." http://www.chazymusictheatre.org/about.html (accessed October 19, 2014).

Clark, Katherine. "Plattsburgh Sister Nominated for NYS Woman of Distinction." http://m.denpubs.com/news/2013/apr/30/plattsburgh-sister-nominated-nys-woman-distinction/ (accessed October 5, 2014).

Clark, Rachel. "Ortloff Secures More Funds for Youth Court." *Press-Republican*, November 28, 2000, http://blog.pressrepublican.com/archive/index.php?option=com_content&view=article&id=4177:ortloff secures_more_funds_for_youth_court&catid=34:news-articles.

Claus, Greg. "Allan Makes History by Preserving It for County." *Press-Republican*, October 20, 1995, 7.

"Clinton County Museum." http://www.clintoncountyhistorical.org/index.html (accessed October 19, 2014).

Clute, Penelope. "Peggy Facto—Murderess or Victim?" *The Historical Society of the Courts of the State of New York* 1.2 (Spring/Summer 2004), http://www.courts.state.ny.us/courts/4jd/plattsburgh_city/facto.shtml accessed 10/9/14.

"CVPH Medical Center: Birthing Center." http://www.cvph.org/specialties/birthing-center/ (accessed October 7, 2014).

"CVPH Medical Center: Champlain Valley Hospital." https://www.cvph.org/about-cvph/history/champlain-valley-hospital.aspx (accessed October 18, 2014).

Davidson, Lucretia Maria. *Amir Khan, and Other Poems: The Remains of Lucretia Maria Davidson, Who Died at Plattsburgh, N.Y., August 27, 1825, Aged 16 years and 11 Months.* New York: G.&C.&H. Carvill, 1829.

Davis, Diana. "County Historian is BPW Woman of the Year." *Press-Republican*, October 22, 1968, 4.

"Distinguished Teaching Professor Sees Art as Language." http://www.plattsburgh.edu/about/profiles/faculty/fine.php (accessed October 17, 2014).

Duprey, Janet. "Inspired to Succeed: Women Who Influenced Our Lives." www.janetduprey.com/inspired.pdf (accessed October 4, 2014).

Dutcher, LaVerne. "Chazy Woman Wins Local History Writing Award." *Press-Republican*, April 5, 1988, 3.

———. "Couple Honored for Service." *Press-Republican*, July 31, 1996, 7.

———. "Historical Collection One for the Record Books." *Press-Republican*, June 20, 1995, 3.

Ellenburg Yesterday and Today. Ellenburg, NY: Court Little Rose #1300 Ellenburg, New York Catholic Daughters of the Americas, 1990.

"English Faculty—Daphne Kutzer." http://web.plattsburgh.edu/academics/english/faculty/kutzer.php (accessed October 17, 2014).

"Entrepreneurship Faculty—Nancy Church." http://web.plattsburgh.edu/academics/entrepreneurship/faculty/church.php (accessed October 17, 2014).

"Events—2014/09/25." http://gsneny.org/events/2014/09/25/women-of-distinction/ (accessed October 5, 2014).

"Events—2013/09/26." http://gsneny.org/events/2013/09/26/women-of-distinction-north/ (accessed October 8, 2014).

Everest, Allan S. *Henry Delord and His Family*. Plattsburgh, NY: The Kent-Delord House Museum, 1979.

———. *The Military Career of Alexander Macomb and Alexander Macomb at Plattsburgh*. Plattsburgh, NY: The Clinton County Historical Association, 1989.

———. *North Country Pioneer: Pliny Moore of Champlain, New York*. Plattsburgh, NY: The Clinton County Historical Association, 1990.

———. *Point au Fer on Lake Champlain*. Plattsburgh, NY: The Clinton County Historical Association, 1992.

———. *Rum Across the Border: The Prohibition Era in Northern New York*. Syracuse, NY: Syracuse University Press, 1978.

"Evergreen Valley Nursing Home." http://www.evergreenvalleynh.com/ (accessed October 19, 2014).

Favreau, Geri. E-mail correspondence with the author, September 5, 2014.

Ford, Fran. *I Will Remember You: A Testament to Both Tenderness of the Human Heart and the Strength of the Human Soul*. Interlaken, NY: Windswept Press, 1994.

Fourth JD—Plattsburgh City Court. http://www.courts.state.ny.us/courts/4jd/plattsburgh_city/facto.shtml (accessed October 9, 2014).

Freedman, Henry K., MD. *From Generation to Generation: The Jewish Congregations of Plattsburgh, N.Y.* Plattsburgh: n.p., 1998.

"Friends of the North Country." http://www.friendsofthenorthcountry.org/ (accessed October 18, 2014).

"Girl Scouts—Facts about Us." https://www.girlscouts.org/who_we_are/facts/ (accessed October 5, 2014).

"Girl Scouts of Northeastern New York announces 2007 Women of Distinction." http://www.denpubs.com/news/2007/oct/20/girl-scouts-of-northeastern-new-york-announces/ (accessed October 8, 2014).

Goss, Carol. "Librarian Thinks Young After 50 Years Service." *Press-Republican*, January 13, 1989, 15.

Harkness, J. Warren, et al. *A History of Peru, New York*. Two volumes. Peru, NY: n.p., 2003.

Harrold, John W. *School Districts in Clinton County, New York*. Plattsburgh, NY: John W. Harrold, 1980.

Havens, Pamela Romeo, ed. *Clinton Community College*. Plattsburgh, NY: Clinton Community College, 1987.

Heart's Delight Farm Heritage Exhibit—The William H. Miner Agricultural Research Institute. http://whminer.org/heritageexhibit.html (accessed October 7, 2014).

Historical Sketches of Plattsburgh, New York, From its First Settlement to Jan. 1, 1893. Reprint, Elizabethtown, NY: Crown Point Press, 1968.

Historical Sketches of the Town of Plattsburgh, 1785–1975. Elizabethtown, NY: Denton Publications, 1975.

"History of St. Augustine's Parish Peru, New York." http://peruparish.org/staugustinehistory.pdf (accessed October 18, 2014).

Holscher, Katie. "Angela Bryant Forrence Remembered for Caring Spirit." *Press-Republican*, June 26, 2005, http://blog.pressrepublican.com/archive/index.php?option=com_content&view=article&id=29204:angela_bryant_forrence_remembered_for_caring_spirit&catid=34:news-articles.

Independent. "Education Is Timeless for AuSable Forks Woman." May 24, 1989.

"Janet Duprey for Assembly." http://janetduprey.com (accessed October 8, 2014).

Kellogg, Dr. David S. *A Doctor at All Hours: The Private Journal of a Small-Town Doctor's Varied Life, 1886–1909*. Edited by Allan S. Everest. Brattleboro, VT: Stephen Greene Press, 1970.

Kemble, Luella North, and Eleanor B. Mayette. *Memories of Honorable Luella R. North: Children's Court Judge of Clinton County, New York—1923–1935*. Plattsburgh, NY: Retired Senior Volunteer Program of Clinton County, 1996.

Kho, Helen Anders. E-mail message to author, August 22, 2014.

"Lady Cougars and Coach Dixon Honored." Last updated March 5, 2012, http://www.clinton.edu/Athletics/Content-news/nid/13632/gid/13/announcement.cml.

Lake Champlain Weekly. Various issues.

Lapensohn, Lee. "Editor's Corner." *Press-Republican*, January 15, 1973, 4.

Little, Gordie. "A Lifetime Partnershipin Community Service." *Strictly Business*, http://www.sbmonthly.com/?p=1045.

———. "Turning Construction into Art: Pat Crosby." *Strictly Business* http://www.sbmonthly.com/?p=1699

LoTemplio, Joe. "City Court Judge Penelope Clute to Leave." *Press Republican*, August 31, 2011, http://www.pressrepublican.com/news/local_news/

article_dd92ac8b-a6b9-5fae-96c1-e52c76797b84.html (accessed October 9, 2014).

Luz, Clayton. "New York Honors Dr. Lucy Hobbs Taylor; Governor's Commission Recognizes Her with Historic Marker." *ADA News*, January 25, 1994, 14.

Manor, Steve. "Woman Honored for Years of Making History." *Press-Republican*, October 12, 1994, 13.

Martin, David Kendall, ed. *The Journal of William Gilliland: 18th Century Pioneer of the Champlain Valley*. Plattsburgh, NY: Clinton County Historical Association, 1997.

Masella, John P., Esq., and Erik Pinsonnault. *Of the People: A History of the Office of the Clinton County District Attorney*. Plattsburgh, NY: A Publication of the Office of the Clinton County District Attorney, 2008.

Mayette, Eleanor B. Written correspondence with the Clinton County Historian's Office, 1998.

A Memoir of Catharine R. Keese, Late of Peru, N.Y. New York: James Egbert, Printer, 1866.

Meyers, Jeff. "Champlain Valley Hospital Celebrates 100th Anniversary." *Press-Republican*, June 20, 2010, http://www.pressrepublican.com/news/local_news/article_2339b3f9-32ee-5a3d-b651-9849418c3069.html?mode=jqm.

"Michelle Davis—Colorado Springs Philharmonic Orchestra." http://csphilharmonic.org/about/musicians/strings/michelle-davis/ (accessed October 19, 2014).

Middleton, Holly, ed. *Sacred Remembrances*. Rouses Point, NY: Border Press, 2013.

"Miner Museum Collection." http://minermuseum.org/alice_dh_collection.html (accessed October 7, 2014).

Minerva, Katie. "Alice T. Miner: The Colonial Revival Movement." *All Points North* (Summer 2013), http://www.apnmag.com.

"Miramichi Chapter 520 OES Honors Charles and Emma Chandler." *The North Countryman* 7 (November 20, 1975).

Monroe, Monica. "OLV Sets New Direction for Graduate's Life," *Press-Republican,* May 31, 1993, 3.

Moore, Suzanne. "Area Women Help Nicaraguan Victims." *Press-Republican*, January 4, 1999, A3.

———. "Catholic Daughters Lauded for Volunteer Work." *Press-Republican*, June 5, 1998, 7.

———. "Local Woman Looking to Complete Book of Historical Church Sketches." *Press-Republican*, November 12, 1997, 8.

———. "Rouses Point Historian Delights in Saving the Past." *Press-Republican,* January 10, 1999, http://blog.pressrepublican.com.

Mowers, Kelly. "Chazy's Musical Set This Weekend." *Press-Republican,* March 7, 1991, 8.

Munafo, James L. *When Duty Calls: A Brief Account of the 100 Year History of the Montgomery Hose, Hood & Ladder Co. #1 of Rouses Point, NY.* Souvenir Edition. Rouses Point, NY: Border Press, 1991.

"National Champs! Women's Hockey Cruises to Third Title in 9–2 Victory over Norwich." http://www.gocardinalsports.com/news/2014/3/22/WHOCKEY_0322141839.aspx?path=whockey (accessed October 20, 2014).

"National Women's Christian Temperance Union (WCTU) Early History." http://www.wctu.org/earlyhistory.html (accessed October 5, 2014).

"North Country Authors." http://www.northcountryauthors.org/authors.php?page=1 (accessed October 19, 2014).

North Country Catholic. "Local Sisters Prepare to Celebrate the May 27 Beatification of Their Foundress Mother St. Louis Mole." http://www.northcountrycatholic.org/Articles/2012/5_23foundress.html (accessed October 16, 2014).

North Countryman. "Grateful for Tournament Help." September 27, 2011. http://www.northcountryman.com/news/2011/sep/27/grateful-tournament-help/.

Old Chazy: Reminscences of Old Chazy Given by Descendants of the Early Settlers at a Literary and Musical Entertainment Held at Academy Hall, Chazy, N.Y. Aug. 23, 1898. Crown Point, NY: Crown Point Press, 1898.

Old Keeseville Tales. Reprint, Elizabethtown, NY: Denton Publications, 1976.

"Our Rabbi—Beth Israel Jewish Congregation." http://www.jcscc.org/about-us/our-rabbisv(accessed October 18, 2014).

Page, Kyle. "Ballantine Takes on New Role in Catholic Education." *North Country Catholic,* http://northcountrycatholic.org/Articles/2011/9_21%20Ballantine.html (accessed October 18, 2014).

Paine, Deborah Coolidge. Written correspondence with the Clinton County Historian's Office, January 12 and 15, 1999.

Palmer, Peter Sailly. *History of Plattsburgh, N.Y., From Its First Settlement to Jan. 1, 1876.* Plattsburgh, NY: n.p., 1877.

Papineau, Jeremiah S. "Plaque Commemorates Local Nursing School History." *Denton Publications,* March 30, 2011, http://www.denpubs.com/news/2011/mar/30/plaque-commemorates-local-nursing-school-history/.

"Paralyzed Veterans Racer Laurie Wood Selected to U.S. Women's Ice Sledge Hockey Team." http://www.pva.org/site/apps/nlnet/content2.aspx?c=ajIRK9NJLcJ2E&b=6350111&ct=14219927 (accessed October 20, 2014).

"Past Exhibitions." http://plattsburgharts.org/?page_id=423 (accessed October 19, 2014).

Peru Daily Gazette. http://www.dailygazette.com.

Peru Gazette. "John Roach Is Laid to Rest." August 29, 2013, http://www.perugazette.com/2013/08/29/john-roach-is-laid-to-rest/.

Plattsburgh Daily Press. "Many Students to Continue Education." September 18, 1937, 3.

———. "No Action in Pal Blade Co. Strike." September 29, 1941, 3.

———. Various issues.

Plattsburgh Daily Republican. "Gold Star Mothers." May 9, 1930, 4.

———. Various issues.

Plattsburgh Press-Republican. "Children's Home of North'n New York Notes Founders' Day Sunday, May 20." May 16, 1951, 8.

———. "Diamond Match Payroll Aids City Economy." January 31, 1956, 7.

———. "825 Pal Blade Employes Strike Today at 3 P.M. As Company Offer Fails." September 20, 1946, 3.

———. "Georgia Harkness U.S. Protestant Representative to Int'l Conclave." August 6, 1946, 3.

———. "Pal Blade Strike Being Continued." November 14, 1944, 3.

———. "Pal Local Meeting Tonight on Strike." September 19, 1946, 3.

———. Various issues.

———. "War Memorial Dedicated in Brief, Solemn Services." December 11, 1950, 3.

Plattsburgh Republican. "Saranac Academy." October 24, 1863, 3.

———. "The Trustees of Plattsburgh Academy." July 7, 1821, 1.

———. Various issues.

Plattsburgh Sentinel and Clinton County Farmer. Various issues.

Plattsburgh Sentinel. "The Gold Star Mothers' Pilgrimage." April 18, 1930, 4.

———. "Reception to Honor City's Gold Star Mothers." June 20, 1930, 4.

———. Various issues.

Porter, Marjorie Lansing. *Plattsburgh 1785–1815–1902*. Burlington, VT: George Little Press, 1964.

Powell, Reverend Lewis N., ed. *Out of the North Country: Christian Pioneers of Northern New York*. Cooperstown: New York State Council of Churches, n.d.

Pratt, Gloria. Correspondence related to Girl Scout Leader of the Year nomination. 1986.

Prero, Mike. "The Story of a Giant: Diamond Match Company (1881–present)." *Hobby History*, July/August 1997, http://www.matrchpro.org/Archives/Hobby%History/Diamond.pdf.

Press-Republican, "Chazy Unit Membership Rowing." February 27, 1981, 50.

———. "CHEERS: to Helen Ianelli." October 2002, http://www.pressrepublican.com.

———. "Davis-Gallagher," October 21, 1986, 8.

———. "Dr. Georgia Harkness." June 11, 1988, 9.

———. "Ellenburg CDA Formed in 1938." February 24, 1984, 51.

———. "Georgia Harkness's Birth to Be Marked." May 4, 1991, 9.

———. "Legal Services Available for Clinton County Elderly." October 17, 1980, 9.

———. "Methodist Meetings Start This Weekend." April 25, 1987, 9.

———. "Mrs. Roach, Peru Teacher, Dies at 41." October 25, 1973, 6.

———. "Musical Production." November 17, 1989, 8.

———. "New Director Steps in at Alice T. Miner Museum." June 15, 2014, http://www.pressrepublican.com.

———. "Parade, Plaque Memorial to Dead." May 30, 1972, 17.

———. "Plattsburgh CDA Formed in '20 with 100 Members." February 27, 1981, 50.

———. "Torch Run Honoring Women to Halt in Plattsburgh." September 9, 1998, 3.

———. "Women in Agriculture Urged to Get Involved." February 15, 1983, 15.

Provost, Frank. "Mrs. Hayes: A Curator for Posterity." *Press-Republican*, March 18, 1961, 9.

"PUMC—United Methodist Women." http://www.plattsburghumc.org/UnitedMethodistWomen.html (accessed October 18, 2014).

Rabideau, Clyde M., ed. *Obituaries*. Plattsburgh, NY: self-published. Editions published 1999–2006.

———. *Vital Statistics*. Plattsburgh, NY: self-published. Editions published 1993–98.

Rennell, Matt. "North Country Mission of Hope." *All Points North* Summer 2006, http://apnmag.com/winter_2006/mission.php.

Republican. Various issues.

"Retirement Dinner Honoring Lois A. Goodspeed, Secretary to the Commander 380th Bombardment Wing (SAC) 21 June 1991," program.

"Riverside Cemetery, Plattsburgh, Clinton County, New York." http://freepages.genealogy.rootsweb.ancestry.com/~frgen/clinton/plattsburgh/riverside_l_z.htm (accessed October 8, 2014).

Ross, John. *This Happened Here*. Rouses Point, NY: Northern Publishing Co., 1955.

Sabourin, Diane. E-mail correspondence with the author, October 13, 2013.

Sexton, Kelly Julian. E-mail correspondence with the author, August 20, 2014.

Shannon, Daniel, and Amanda Shannon Frennier. E-mail correspondence with the author, October 21, 2014.

Shields, Addie Lawrence. Resume on file at the Clinton County Historian's Office, 1998.

Sixty-four Campuses: The State University of New York to 1985. Albany, NY: Office of University Affairs and Development, 1985.

Skopp, Douglas R. *Bright with Promise: From the Normal and Training School to SUNY Plattsburgh, 1889–1989, A Pictorial History*. Norfolk, VA: Donning Company, 1989.

Smith, Anne. "Youth Orchestra Unveils String Training Ensemble." *Press-Republican*, April 2, 1993, 6.

Souvenir Industrial Edition of Plattsburgh 1897. Reprint, Burlington, VT: Cornerstone Bookshop, 1978.

Spissinger, Jessica, and Kristi Spissinger O'Connor. E-mail correspondence with the author, October 24, 2014.

Spring, Louise. "Active in Body, Mind and Spirit." *Press-Republican*, January 13, 1999, A6.

Sullivan, Nell Jane Barnett, and David Kendall Martin. *A History of the Town of Chazy, Clinton County, New York*. Burlington, VT: George Little Press, 1970.

Sunderland, Lincoln, ed. *History of Peru, New York*. Peru, NY: Bicentennial Committee of Peru, 2003.

Taylor, Sister Mary Christine. *A History of Catholicism in the North Country*. Camden, NY: A.M. Farnsworth Sons, 1972.

"Temple Beth Israel, Plattsburgh, NY." http://www.bethisraelplattsburgh.org/community/sisterhood/ (accessed October 9, 2014).

Town of Clinton. Clinton, NY: Bicentennial Committee of the Town of Clinton, 1976.

"Town of Schuyler Falls Sesqui-centennial 1848–1948." Schuyler Falls, NY: Town of Schuyler Falls, 1998.

Trudeau, Doris Brown. Papers, Clinton County Historian's Office.

Tuling, Rabbi Kari. "Why I'm Going to Israel for Women of the Wall." http://ravblog.ccarnet.org/2013/11/why-im-going-to-israel-for-women-of-the-wall/ (accessed October 18, 2014).

Tuttle, Mrs. George Fuller. *Three Centuries in Champlain Valley: A Collection of Historical Facts and Incidents*. Plattsburgh, NY: Saranac Chapter, DAR, 1909.

"United Methodist Women." http://www.unitedmethodistwomen.org/about (accessed October 18, 2014).

"United States Constitution." http://www.archives.gov/exhibits/charters/constitution_amendments_11-27.html#18 (accessed October 16, 2014).

Westbrook, Virginia. *A Thoroughly Wide Awake Little Village: A Walking Guide to Keeseville's Historic District*. Keeseville, NY: Friends of the North Country, 1996.

West, Mae H., ed. *Stat*. Plattsburgh, NY: Physicians Hospital, 1931.

White, Myra Magoon. *History of the Town of Ellenburg Clinton County New York*. Ellenburg, NY: Ellenburg Kiwanis Club, 2001.

"Will Safety Razor Firm Reconsider?" December 12, 1953, 1.

Winans, Maggie, ed. *Clinton County: I Remember When*. Elizabethtown, NY: Senior Citizens Council of Clinton County, 1983.

Winslow, Edmund J. "Local Historians in New York State." Originally published January 1982, accessed October 19, 2014, https://www.nysm.nysed.gov/services/historian/winslowdoc.html.

Women of Courage: Ten North Country Pioneers in Profile. St. Lawrence County, NY: American Association of University Women, 1989.

"Women of Distinction." http://mountainlake.org/events/women-of-distinction/ (accessed October 15, 2014).

Wright, Gerianne. "SUNY Plattsburgh Geologist Named SUNY Distinguished Teaching Professor." *CallingCard*, June 2013, http://www.plattsburgh.edu/alumni/newsletter/june2013/roden-tice.php.

INDEX

V

W

ABOUT THE AUTHOR

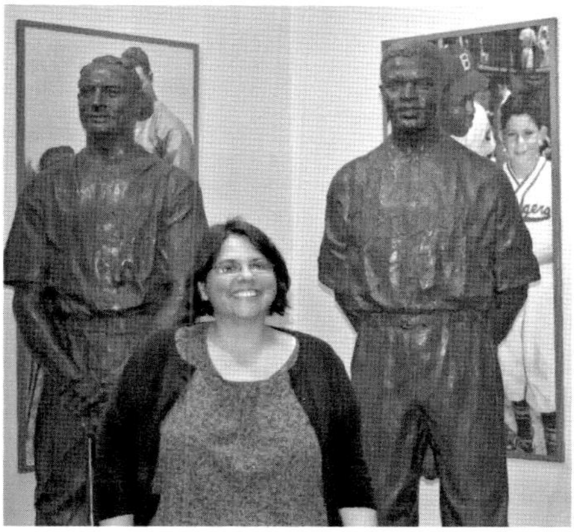

Anastasia L. Pratt grew up in Plattsburgh, New York, and attended Peru Central School. After graduating in 1994, she continued her education at Plattsburgh State University, earning a BA in history (summa cum laude), and at the University of Michigan, where she earned both an MA and PhD in American culture. Pratt serves as the Clinton County historian, helping to preserve, organize and disseminate local history. She is also an assistant professor at SUNY Empire State College and the coordinator of the school's Advanced Certificate in Public History.

In addition to her historical work, Anastasia is a double bassist who plays with a variety of local orchestras and an avid reader. She lives in Plattsburgh with her family.

Visit us at
www.historypress.net

This title is also available as an e-book